CW00558684

Al

Turing

The Life And Legacy Of The English
Computer Scientist

*(The Incredible True Story Of The Man Who
Cracked The Cod)*

Leroy Byers

Published By **Zoe Lawson**

Leroy Byers

Alan Turing: The Life And Legacy Of The English Computer Scientist (The Incredible True Story Of The Man Who Cracked The Cod)

ISBN   978-1-77485-618-5

No part of this guidebook shall be reproduced in any form without permission in writing from the publisher except in the case of brief quotations embodied in critical articles or reviews.

Legal & Disclaimer

The information contained in this ebook is not designed to replace or take the place of any form of medicine or professional medical advice. The information in this ebook has been provided for educational & entertainment purposes only.

The information contained in this book has been compiled from sources deemed reliable, and it is accurate to the best of the Author's knowledge; however, the Author cannot guarantee its accuracy and validity and cannot be held liable for any errors or omissions. Changes are periodically made to this book. You must consult your doctor or get professional medical advice before using any of the suggested remedies, techniques, or information in this book.

Upon using the information contained in this book, you agree to hold harmless the Author from and against any damages, costs, and expenses, including any legal fees potentially resulting from the application of any of the information provided by this guide. This disclaimer applies to any damages or injury caused by the use and application, whether directly or

Table of Contents

Contents

Chapter 1: Secret Whispers

Marcus Cicero (Roman lawyer and statesman) once said "Nervos belle, pecuniam unlimitedam" – "The sinews are war, unlimited cash." Waging war can be a costly enterprise. The British Empire was nearly bankrupt in 1941. They were fighting against Nazi Germany and their relentless expansion across Europe. Britain was left to its own devices, with no support from the USA.

However, war is more than just a body. It needs a nervous and communication system to transmit commands from commanders (the brain) to the armored feet that will carry them. It is vital that the enemy doesn't be able read these commands. Otherwise, they will know what you expect. This could have a major impact on the outcome of the war. The enemy will know everything you have planned before it happens. The nerves are secure communications. With nearly 2,000 miles between the Spanish border and Moscow and with submarines operating all the way to the US coastline, the Nazis faced huge challenges in communicating secretly.

It was a challenging task that they met with typical German efficiency and innovation. In every major headquarters, at every U-Boat or warship, was a wooden box varnished with wood. A complex electromechanical device was contained inside. It could make plain text a gibberish stream random-seeming alphabets, or restore the meaning of an incoming encrypted message. This was known as the Enigma machine. Germany produced more than 40,000. Throughout the war, millions of messages were generated, each message encyphered using a fiendishly complex and changing transmutation.

It was not a new invention to use a cipher machine. Substitution tables are a tradition that dates back thousands upon thousands of year. Thomas Jefferson also invented the Jefferson Wheel which was still in use with the US Army till 1945. Enigma was distinguished by its complicated mechanism and numerous transformations that it imposed upon the text. Even the simplest military machine was capable of changing each letter nine-times as it went through the circuits. With every key press, the machine would reconfigure itself so that the next one would be encoded in a completely other cypher. Even if a machine fell in the hands of British forces, it would still work but without the key settings that change every day. The British must be able to determine how the machine was set-up in order to read an intercepted message. If it is not, it will simply produce more gibberish. Guessing the settings was hopeless - there were 1,074,584,913,000,000,000,000,000 possible start configurations and only one of them would work. It is not surprising that Germans believed Enigma was unbreakable until the end.

But they were wrong. They did not know it had been cracked before 1932. This was an older model that was simpler. A brilliant team from the Polish Cypher Bureau discovered a weakness in the system, and they managed to exploit it. Although the work was difficult and time-consuming, Enigma could still be solved with luck. The machines, as well as the operating procedures, were improved by 1939 when the war broke out. The volume and speed of the messages was increasing rapidly, and even though the Polish had automated the process with machines, their methods were still slow enough to manage the traffic.

But the British were able to decode messages using their own methods, something that was not known by the Nazis (and almost everyone else until the 1970s). The British had already made several breakthroughs in 1941 that had cracked the Enigma encryption cypher. They were now able decode messages on an industrial level. These breakthroughs weren't made possible by a commando raid and espionage mission to steal Enigma's secrets. They were achieved by a group composed of university professors. Telephone engineers. Crossword lovers. This strange group was driven by one man. He was a mild-mannered, eccentric mathematics professor from the University of Cambridge. This man was an undeniable genius whose late life was filled with tragedy and controversy. He probably played a greater part in the eventual Allied victory. His contribution towards the war effort was only recently recognized. Most people have heard of Churchill (and Eisenhower), Montgomery, Patton or even de Gaulle. But many are unfamiliar with Alan Turing.

Chapter 2: Schol Days

The British Empire, at its peak of size and power, was in the beginning 20th century. Around 25% of the world's surface was either British colonies or British dominions. From Canada to Cape Town to Hong Kong and the Falkland Islands, in the South Atlantic, the Union Flag flew. India, a vast country with abundant resources and a large population, is the jewel in this crown. The Indian government was the ultimate authority, but the country was independent. India's civil service was made up of both British and Indian officials. Although strong ties were formed between colonists of India and the natives, they each started to adapt to the other's culture. The British love to eat curry and the British tradition that polo is played by the upper classes of India date back to this time. India's civil and military services follow the British model but each retains their own identity. Many Britons who worked in distant Raj provinces had to rely on the fact that they were born in their home country for their identities. Ethel Turing gave birth to her second son in 1912 and her husband Julius took a leave from Chatrapur in India. The couple then made the long journey by sea back to England. It was a chance for them to spend time with John their older son. John was living with a retired British Army soldier and his wife at Hastings. The family rented Maida Vale, a house in London, and prepared for their baby.

2 Warrington Crescent, Maida Vale is now the Colonnade Hotel. The Colonnade attracted many famous guests over time, including John F. Kennedy. [1] Sigmund F. Reud, an actor and musician, was also a frequent guest. The Colonnade is a Victorian building in brick and Portland stone that looks elegant and luxurious. It started out as two large, brick-built town houses in 1865. In the end, it became a boarding house and then, Warrington Lodge, a medical and surgical home for women. [2] It became a Hotel in 1935.

Ethel Turing went to labor on June 23, 1912; her husband called taxis to take her to Warrington Lodge. Ethel Turing was able to give birth to a healthy baby boy that same day. Julius Turing also named him Alan Mathison Turing.

Julius had taken extended leaves to travel to London to be with his wife. He still held a Chatrapur post, and eventually had to return. The elder Turings had long discussions about how to handle the matter. Julius was to return to India with his family and go to England whenever possible. They thought that it would give their sons an "normal" education, rather than returning to India as family. Chitrapur was Orissa and Bihar's colonial headquarter. This is a remote part of northeast India, bordering Bangladesh. They could go school and make friends in England.

Ethel moved in Hastings to be with the boys and began to care for them. Ethel began to notice characteristics in Alan that were different from her brother. He was an extremely inquisitive child from a young age. This was sometimes mistaken for mischief. He connected things and was open to new ideas. Ethel saw him "planting" broken toys, after he had seen his mother planting seeds. However, he probably thought Ethel was seeing it as him trying to hide evidence. He also learned other skills fast; he could learn to read in three weeks. He took an immediate and passionate interest in numbers when he was young and loved the way that they could all be organized into sequences. Alan kept stopping at every lamp that he saw to verify the serial number. He found out that Hastings' street lamps had all been stamped with an iron number. As a preschooler, he already knew how numbers worked together. It would become a lifelong interest.

Alan's parents took him to St. Michael's in Hastings when he was six. They were a private elementary school in St. Leonard's. St. Michael's School closed years ago, however, the Victorian townhouse building that housed it still stands at 20 Charles Road. While the house is big enough to be used for a residence, the school is small enough to serve as a school. That was common for private schools of the time. Because the school was small, teachers were able to give more attention and focus on individual students. Turing was quickly recognized by his headmistress as an exceptionally intelligent boy. Ethel had chosen St. Michael's to teach Alan Latin. Although he was proficient in all subjects and excelled in math, his unique aptitude was for mathematics.

Schools - at least the good ones - offer much more than just knowledge or critical thinking. They socialize their students and Turing's character started to emerge during his time at St. Michael's. Although he was highly intelligent, he was also quite shy. He never learned to overcome this. He became passionate about fairness, and he used rules from a young age to help him achieve it. He also seemed to find rules comforting. However, he quickly became infuriated when they were violated, even if they were his own creations. Ethel was reading John Bunyan's The Pilgrim's Progress while Ethel was still a little boy. It is incredible that Ethel would read such complex and nuanced material to a young boy. Because of its complexity and multifaceted meanings, it is difficult to believe. Alan immediately protested when she suggested that she leave out some of her more difficult theology. He believed skipping portions was against the "rules" of reading, and the story was destroyed.

Alan moved to Hazelhurst School at the age of ten. It was a preparatory high school situated just outside Frant (which is twenty miles north-east of Hastings). Ethel moved to Hazelhurst as a boarding house, with her two sons there. Ethel also began to spend more time in India, with Julius. Alan kept them busy with his constant stream of letters. These letters contained ideas that he had for improving typewriters or fountain pens. His father replied encouragingly with suggestions for new experiments. A father's suggestion led him to borrow some surveying equipment. This allowed him to measure the heights the trees were growing on school grounds. Turing, unlike many mathematicians that think in abstractions of pure numbers, was able bridging this gap to bring his thoughts back into the real world and to use his abilities to solve real issues. This is something every engineer does, but it is rare in a mathematician with the level Turing would achieve.

Hazelhurst wasn't the right place for him. The school's objectives were very classical. They sought to create well-rounded citizens of society who could properly decline Latin verbs and write grammatically correct sentences. Science and mathematics were not prominently included in the curriculum. The boys took a course in basic calculus. However, he excelled in sports, even if he was easily distracted. Ethel created a sketch of Turing in spring 1923. It shows him, with his field hockey stick in the hand, staring at a daisy, while his teammates fight for their ball.

Turing was thirteen when he left preparatory school. His next destination was Sherborne. [1] It's an old public school in the small Dorset place of the name. Sherborne was founded in the early

8th-century by Saint Aldhelm. Today, the school houses the remains from the Benedictine monastery it was associated in the 10th-16th century. Sherborne was an old boarding school. Like Hazelhurst it focused on classical education. It also prepared boys to attend university with the expectation of being able to get into Oxford and Cambridge. Turing was excited about the prospect of going to such a high-profile school. But, it wasn't an easy path.

Britain was the world's largest producer and exporter for coal during the first half the 20th. The 1920s saw the production decline as other countries increased their exports of coal and provided supplies to markets that had been buying it from Britain. Falling profits led miners to lower wages. The Trades Union Congress, a powerful union representing mineworkers, demanded subsidies from the government for their pay packets. TUC demanded that the temporary subsidy for one month be made permanent. Unfortunately for them the government had already used the month to prepare but felt it was in strong enough form to deny the union demands. Britain's last general strike started on May 3, 1926. It collapsed in just ten day as volunteers took charge of the essential services. However from May 3 to 13 there were severe disruptions in heavy manufacturing and transport.

Turing didn't like this because Sherborne had started a new term on May 3rd and the family was now living 60 miles away in Southampton. Transport workers had come out in solidarity with the miners. No buses and trains were available. Ethel couldn't drive so it looked like Alan wouldn't make it to school until the strike ended. He was determined, but that was a great underestimation. He was a strong cyclist so he decided to travel on his bicycle. He was fully loaded with clothes and books, and had miles of country roads to navigate. He made it. He started his journey on Sunday, May 2, and it took him 2 days. He stayed overnight in a hotel close to Shaftesbury, and continued his journey the following morning. Alan Turing was there to assist Sherborne's new students as they waited for their registrations late on Monday afternoon.

Unfortunately, academically, his time at Sherborne was not as successful. He struggled to master the subjects the school emphasized. In his third and fourth years, he was last in English and first in Latin. He annoyed his teachers even in math and science by trying to ignore their tasks and looking for things he thought was more interesting. He was actually progressing at a rate that his teachers probably couldn't understand. While he was still shy, he rarely spent time with the other boys in year. Instead, he was always in the library and reading voraciously. Two years after his arrival at Sherborne he was having informal study sessions and he found a book that he thought shouldn't even be in the school library. A young professor at Berlin Academy of Sciences published it in German in 1916. His advanced concepts of Physics were not accessible to most people at that time. The English translation was of Albert Einstein's Relativitat.

In 1928, physics was still dominated primarily by classical mechanics. Relativity, Einstein's first book, was completely exempt from these laws. He didn't want it to be considered an academic publication for researchers and professors. Instead, the book was intended to be read by a broad audience. It was a roughly equal to Stephen Hawking's 1988 A Brief History of Time. Einstein hoped it would increase understanding of his work. He didn't want the book to be controversial and so he left out some his thoughts on Newtonian physics.

Turing wasn't fooled enough, he didn't leave enough. Understanding the book requires reading it. The message Einstein was leaving behind was clear to the teenager: the German scientist believed Newton had been mistaken. Einstein seems have been relying on the fact that everyone accepts Newton's law without question to cover this fact. However, Turing with his natural curiosity didn't agree to anything and he soon realized that many Einstein experiments and equations were created to test Newton's laws. Why would they? Turing could only see one possibility in the nature tests. Einstein doubted that the basic principles of physics had been supported for more than 300 year. His deduction was completely correct. [5]

Turing could easily pick up Einstein's doubts. Because he had a truly wide mind, he wasn't credulous. But he was open to challenging and reconsidering even the things he believed. He did not believe that something was true because of the person who said it. Newton's laws have been accepted over the centuries and were sufficient for most purposes. NASA sent Apollo 11 on its first mission to the Moon in 1969. NASA used Newtonian calculations to calculate their mission. However, new research would show that they were wrong. Turing's tendency to be a tyrant was evident to Einstein, who reformulated one of his equations from the book to make them more understandable. He also devised Einstein's geodesic equation of motion.

Turing was admitted to Sherborne's Sixth Year in the same year that Einstein discovered his work. This two-year period is when English students usually study for and sit the exams that determine if they can apply to university. In 1928, this was called the Higher School Certificate. Although Fifth Form School Certificates were intended to be generalist qualifications, students in Sixth Form were allowed more specialized training. Turing also weighted his courses towards his most favorite areas of science, mathematics, and other sciences. This was to make this shy but brilliant boy one of the most important people in his life.

Christopher Morcom was one ahead but Turing was in the Sixth and they were now sharing some of the exact same classes. Turing had seen Morcom outside the school, and was struck at his appearance. It was this hint of samesex attraction that he later found to be the first sign that Morcom was gay. Morcom was small, thin and light for his age. This contrasted to Turing who was muscular and athletic. Morcom was also plagued with illnesses. Turing noticed that in 1927 Morcom had gone to school but returned looking thin and drawn. Morcom was a bright, confident boy. Turing, however, had never been able to get into a conversation. After realizing they had a mutual passion for math and science, he overcame his reservations and approached him. They soon became friends, sharing a common interest which they could talk about for hours.

In 1929 Turing reached the Upper Sixth. This was the final stage of the much-feared Higher Certificate exams. Morcom was still in his Upper Sixth class due to frequent illness. Turing worked with his friend to make it possible for him to sit next to him. They solved problems together often much earlier than what the school had given them. Turing's original school notebook pages show that while they were supposed learn French, they were actually discussing advanced concepts in Euclidian Geometry and playing tic tac-toe.

Turing was shocked by Morcom's friendship. He had been shy and quiet his entire life. However, suddenly he found someone with whom he could communicate his thoughts. Although he was naturally attracted physically to the older boy he enjoyed the sharing of thoughts. Turing talked about Pi with someone who was not afraid to discuss it. There was someone who shared his enthusiasm and knowledge of Einstein's theories. Morcom also taught him the art of intellectual discipline. Turing had an insatiable passion for the subjects which interested him, but his work wasn't always well-organized. Morcom had a different approach. He carefully passed this on. Turing, eager for success, worked hard learning these crucial lessons. His success is evident. His schoolwork began to improve beyond all recognition. This was a result of a new methodical approach to problem-solving that astonished his teachers. His math and science grades had always been low due to sloppy work and cutting corners. However, he has become more focused. His intelligence, energy and intellect were now being refined into something truly impressive.

Turing and Morcom made a trip to Cambridge, England in December 1929. Many universities only accept students based primarily on their Higher Certificate results. But, Oxbridge's elite colleges saw this as the first hurdle. All applicants who achieved a satisfactory grade in school had to then take university entrance exams. Both teenagers wanted to succeed in the process and receive admission to study math. Turing even wrote that he was as excited about the idea of spending one week with Morcom, as he is about Cambridge. [6] However, he was prepared for the exam as well as the interview. However, the pair stopped by London first. They visited Morcom's mom at her sculpture studio, where they "helped" her to create a marble bust. Then, they took the train up to Cambridge.

The trip was not without its challenges. Morcom was offered a scholarship as well as a place at Trinity College. Turing, however, didn't make it. This was a serious blow, but it wasn't fatal. However, public schools allowed students to continue studying for the exams for an extra year so that he could retake them in 1930. Although he might be one year behind Morcom in getting to Cambridge, he would make it there and the two of them could continue their friendship through shared interests in science.

He didn't know the tragedy was only around the corner.

Before the invention of antibiotics tuberculosis remained a serious illness in advanced countries. Although plagues like cholera have been eliminated from British towns by improvements in hygiene, it is possible that any cough or sneeze could be a carrier of the deadly Mycobacterium tuberculosis. Once you are infected, there is no cure. Protect your scarred lungs from any pollution. Many people eventually died from their disease. Others died quickly as the infection weakened the pulmonary blood vessels and eventually caused irreversible internal bleeding. Children were the most at-risk. Not only were there the usual human forms of the disease that were spread through exhaled particles, but also the bovine form, which was transmitted by droplets of air. Up to 40% were infected in Britain. The bacteria can sometimes get into the milk, and until pasteurization became more common, it was possible for one drink to transmit the disease. Chris Morcom had been absent from school for a while due to bovineTB. Before pasteurization, one drink could transmit the bacteria. [7]

Turing was devastated. After many lonely years in school, Turing had finally found companionship. However, it was suddenly taken from him. This was a crushing blow that broke many of his beliefs. He was an ordinary, low-key Church of England believer up until this point. He found that he was no longer able to accept the idea a supreme God would allow such a savage death. His grief and anger destroyed his faith. He was a fervent atheist the rest of life. However, he never abandoned the idea of mind-body separation. Three days after Morcom was killed, he wrote to the mother to say that he was certain of meeting him again. A long letter to Morcom in 1932 reiterated this belief. He believed that the spirit could survive, but his beliefs were quite different to those of Christianity. His later work was influenced greatly by them. He wrote "Personally I believe spirit is really eternally related with matter," but it wasn't always by the same type of body. It would then raise a fascinating question, could spirit be found in a computer?

Turing was still as distraught by Morcoms's death as he was when he died. However, Turing slowly began to feel better and he returned to Cambridge in Dec 1930. He did a better job in the interview and was given a place at King's College. He spent some more time at Sherborne. After a lengthy summer vacation, he packed everything again and headed to Cambridge.

Chapter 3: Cambridge

Turing had struggled with school because of the constant buzz of being surrounded hundreds of other boys, tight managed study and constrained expectations about what students should be learning. His intelligence and Morcom's guidance had enabled him to persevere, but it had been difficult for him. The fact that he was gay slowly dawned upon him - a tremendous stigma in the more conservative society of the day - must have caused him to suffer internal conflicts.

He found himself in an entirely new environment. King's was not like the schools he had attended. The first female students didn't get in until 1972. It was a distinctly masculine campus with strong traditions of sports and an atmosphere of pure academic enquiry that fit Turing perfectly. It was also a relatively closed society. The college was an autonomous entity within the University of Cambridge. And its inhabitants were protected greatly from the rest of the nation. All lifestyles, including eccentricities, shyness, and unconventional lifestyles, were tolerated by the tutors. But, what was most important, they expected students to focus on their chosen field. King's College was not going to criticize Turing's ignoring of French verbs. But if Turing wanted to focus solely on ever more advanced mathematics that was fine.

Modern universities often house thousands of students on large campuses. They are taught in large halls. They eat in cafeterias, local fast food joints, and they live in student residences. Cambridge was very different in the 1930s. There were only a few hundred undergraduates in 1930s Cambridge. Today there are 420. This college was more tranquil and intimate. Students shared large, private rooms within the college buildings. Then they ate together in a grand hall. Lectures could only have a dozen students. Less work was done in individual sessions or in tutoring sessions. Degrees were more open-ended, with students at all levels of their degrees able to pursue their own interests much more easily than they can now. In a professor's private room or at one of the college bars, students, undergrads, and academics could socialize together. Many were retired Army NCOs who ensured their young charges got their mail. A large domestic staff also took care of their housekeeping. The college's microsociety had a lot of tolerance and was largely unaffected by the conservatism of the British public. The way that a student felt attracted was to other men. King's College faculty and students were not going be overly excited about it. Turing's true potential was realized at King's College with this sudden freedom.

Turing was moving forward in mathematics and science since 1932. He now had a strong foundation in relativity, which accurately describes how large objects behave. Turing was also able to discover quantum mechanics through John Von Neumann's research. This is a new science field that started with studying light's behavior, and now covers the behavior at the subatomic scale. Modern electronics and microprocessors work on quantum principles. Turing thought quantum mechanics was the key to understanding the link between mind, matter, and energy. He began his work in 1933 on Principia Mathematica from Bertrand Russell.

Russell was a former Cambridge lecturer. He'd been expelled from Trinity College after expressing pacifist views. After he returned to Cambridge as an interested socialist, he went to the Soviet Union for "sexual irrationality" and got into trouble in the USA. However, he was still influential at Cambridge. The Oxbridge universities are known for their antiestablishment beliefs. In fact some of Britain's most infamous traitors – Philby, Blunt Burgess and Maclean-- were recruited there by Soviets in early 1930s. Turing was only an undergraduate. Blunt (and Burgess) were both gay. Maclean, on the other hand, was bisexual. There also was overlap between the circle openly gay students as well as the leftist groups. Turing had a romantic relationship with the antiwar movement which Russell and other academics supported. However, Turing stayed away from Marxism and his undergraduate politics were center-left. He wasn't a communist and did not have any sympathies towards the USSR. Turing was also a complete maths enthusiast, so the NKVD shadowy recruitment agents would likely have overlooked him. The Soviet Union was home to many outstanding mathematicians. However, the intelligence agency was more interested to see who was planning to join British government.

Turing wasn't likely to be drawn into the Soviets web even though he was of interest. His less radical politics and his aversion to the gay scene were just two of his many attributes. While he was able to accept his homosexuality at Cambridge and had some brief affairs with James Atkins (a fellow mathematician), he didn't fit into that particular group. Turing was much more into athletics than the other gay undergraduates. He was tall, muscular, and in excellent physical condition by this point. He eagerly joined the college's sporting events. Running was his passion. He also learned to row, an Oxbridge classic, and later to sail a dinghie. Atkins, his lover, discussed Tolstoy while drinking sherry in someone's study. Turing, on the other hand, was more likely out on the River Cam, legs and back straining, as he helped to propel one the eight-oar, fast boats.

He was also dedicating as much time to his degree. With his final exams coming up in the late 1930s and early 1934, he began to combine all he'd learned into a thorough understanding of the highly specialized subject. The effort paid off. In 1934, he received an honors first-class degree in mathematics. Now, he needed to decide what to pursue next.

He ended up choosing the simplest option, and just stayed in Cambridge. He lived another year in King's College, continuing his research and writing a dissertation, which he hoped would secure him a permanent job at the university. Now he was working on the central limits theorem. The theorem says that if enough random numbers (or more) are analyzed and collected, they will form "normal distributions" which is commonly called a bell curve. Turing had set out to prove this theorem. It was discovered twelve years ago by Jarl Waldemar Lindeberg, a Finnish mathematician. Turing's work could have been rendered useless by this, as a dissertation should be considered original research. But, he was blessed. The college was impressed enough to accept Turing's paper when he presented it. Turing was elected a Fellow at King's College in 1935.

Most universities consider a fellow a researcher, junior teaching faculty or a professor. At Oxbridge they are a member of the college's governing committee. For anyone interested in academic careers, they have many privileges. Two of the most valuable are the privileges to eat at college's top table along with the staff and the possibility to stay free. Turing was now in a position to pursue his research with the help of a suite comprising a bedroom and bathroom as well as guaranteed meals. In return for a modest income, he was expected help tutor students. But the rest was his. He had many ideas to fill it.

Math can have profound implications for many people, even though it is hard for most people to get excited. David Hilbert, who was a professor at Gottingen University in Germany, was one the most exciting early 20th-century mathematicians. Hilbert's Hotel is a model that explains infinity. This was one of Hilbert's specialties. This slightly bizarre model shows the implications that limitless numbers can be explained by a hotel with infinite rooms. They're also full when you get there. Hilbert's genius lies in taking concepts that don't make sense and making them real-world problems that everyone can relate to. Hilbert's Hotel has a manager who can quickly find you a place. He simply needs to ask all of the guests to move up one floor. The person in Room 1 moves into Room 2, the person in Room 2 moves into Room 3 and so on; the person in Room 1,274,974,230,643,021 moves into 1,274,974,230,643,022. There is still Room 1.

Hilbert then went on to describe how to find rooms suitable for any number or guests. (If there are n people, you need to move existing guests up n numbers), and even how it can be used to accommodate an infinite number. It wasn't easy for advanced math to be fun but he made it easy. Turing loved his approach and was interested in the challenges he presented to his peers. One of these, devised by Hilbert in 1928, went by the forbidding German name of Entscheidungsproblem.

The Decisionsproblem or the Decision Problem is a fiendishly mashup of logic and math. To solve this problem, an algorithm must be able to decide whether or not a mathematical assertion is valid for all purposes. Its use in daily life is negligible, but Hilbert enjoys setting problems and Turing has quietly become one of Britain's foremost mathematicians. He spent nearly a decade working on the Entscheidungsproblem and finally reached his conclusion. He presented his paper, April 1936 to Professor M.H.A. Newman, who had pointed Newman to the problem in first place, was told for the second occasion in his short career that he'd lost. Newman received just a paper from Alonzo Christian, an American mathematician. He also concluded that it was impossible to solve the problem. Turing was required to reference Church's work and his paper was delayed until August. Church won the competition to solve Hilbert's puzzle. Church-Turing was the final solution to the Entscheidungsproblem. The young Englishman's paper proved to be far more significant than the one Church had originally proposed. Church had solved the problem using theoretical math assumptions; his solution relied solely on paper. Turing had originally tried to simplify and restate a problem that Kurt Godel had attempted, but changed his mind. He started to look at ways to solve his Entscheidungsproblem. These devices, which he envisioned would be fed information by a punched-paper tape, he named A-Machines. Modern mathematicians give credit where they are due. They call hypothetical versions, still in use in many research projects, Turing Machines. They also have a name for those which aren't hypothetical and actually exist. We call them computers.

Chapter 4: Princeton

Turing was likely influenced perhaps by his views on matter, spirit and the possibility of computers that can process information. Calculating machines, and even primitive computer programs, existed long before Turing. Charles Babbage's plans for a programmable Difference Engine were published in 1822 by Charles Babbage. Battleships of the Royal Navy had been fitted with electromechanical control computers since the First World War. The Turing Machine was a different concept. Turing also referred to it as the Universal Machine. He envisioned a device that, if programmed correctly, could calculate any thing that could possibly be computed. It was useful for mathematicians because it was a possible device. Turing wasn't content with hypotheticals. Turing was determined to make his vision come true. He decided that the best option was to visit the USA.

There has been a long history between British and US universities. Both students and faculty can cross the Atlantic in a short time due to their shared language and academic cultures. Turing traveled to Princeton University, September 1936 to study under Alonzo.

It was a mutually beneficial partnership. Church had been an instructor at Princeton for nine year and had extensive knowledge in computational theory. Turing, although younger and less experienced, was a gifted researcher who could make ingenious discoveries and take deductions. Their relationship seemed to be strained. Church described Turing in a "rather eccentric" way as a loner. While the Englishman was very shy, he had a lively social life at the graduate school. Alonzo, however, was left out. Things were much more pleasant in the classroom. Between them they explored further into their answers to the Entscheidungsproblem, refining their joint thesis that's still the standard explanation to Hilbert's challenge. Turing also began work on a functional, working version a primitive computing machine. His PhD was returned to England in 1938. Turing also took with him a circuitboard that held three of the four necessary stages. His PhD dissertation emphasized machine computing, with complex issues such the "halting" problem. This was something he'd first mentioned while working at Cambridge. Is it possible to tell whether a Turing Machine will ever finish its program, or just keep going forever, if it is being set to work with one set of inputs? Turing determined that it doesn't. He developed the idea of "oracles", an additional processor that could answer this, and many other questions at Princeton. His oracles were in some ways similar to modern selftest programs. But, in 1938, they were clearly mathematical models intended to assist with advanced calculations. They were fake.

Turing also had another reason at this point to work towards making his ideas reality. Church and his colleagues at Princeton didn't know this, but he was discreetly approached by a British intelligence organization before he went to the USA. They were keen to see his work and he secretly agreed to collaborate with them. They were curious about how a Turing Machine could be used to solve specific types of algorithms. Turing's brain didn't need to be as sharp as his to see what they meant. The group was called GC&CS for Government Code and Cypher School.

Turing settled quickly back into Cambridge after Princeton. King's College was his safe haven, giving him the time and freedom to do his work. He marked essays, tutored college students, built his prototype machine, ran endless miles in flat Cambridgeshire, and even wrote essays. He also sat through any lecture that could enhance his already remarkable knowledge of maths. Ludwig Wittgenstein gave some of these. This was Ludwig Wittgenstein. A Jewish Austrian aristocrat who had been studying at Cambridge since 1912. He fought in the First World War for the Austro-Hungarian Empire and later gained British citizenship. He had been a Trinity College Fellow for many years and was elected to be a professor there of philosophy in 1939. Turing was curious to hear about his thoughts on the logical base of mathematics. Turing was less interested when he heard his views. Wittgenstein believed mathematical concepts could only be invented by mathematicians. Turing believed mathematics could discover absolute truths. The two discussed the matter and then argued. Turing was impressed by Wittgenstein's intellect and remained convinced of his mistakes.

Turing was convinced, by September 1938, that mathematics must produce absolute truths. He spoke with GC&CS after his return to Princeton. They discussed what he had learned from the USA. The British interest was growing in cryptanalysis, breaking codes. Nazi Germany had reoccupied Rhineland that had been demilitarized from the First World War. Germany annexed Austria by Germany in March 1938. There was little protest, and Hitler began to inflame a crisis about the Sudetenland of Czechoslovakia. This region was home to a large number of ethnic Germans. They were eager to become part of the Third Reich's growing empire, but the Czechoslovak government refused to give up its territory. At the end of the summer, Nazis living in the Sudetenland wanted union with Germany. The British prime minister Neville Chamberlain was involved in attempts to negotiate a settlement. Chamberlain believed that by accommodating Hitler's demands – not all of which were unreasonable, the Rhineland having been extensively pillaged in France for instance - it would be possible avoid another European war. Others in Britain were more realistic. The military thought appeasement would be enough to allow them time to start fighting. A large rearmament programme was already in place. The top brass and intelligence services believed war was inevitable. They wanted every advantage they could. One key advantage would be the ability read the signals of the enemy, something the British had achieved with success in the previous war. They wanted to replicate this feat this time around.

But there was an issue.

Chapter 5: Enigma

Arthur Scherbius is a Frankfurt-am-Main-born engineer. He was born October 20, 1878. He completed his studies in the rapidly growing field of electricity at university in Munich, Hannover, and was awarded an electrical engineering doctorate in 1904. He was a competent, but not extraordinary engineer who worked for fourteen years designing turbines. He also invented some unusual inventions, such as the electric pillow. Scherbius & Ritter, his own company, was founded in February 1918. They patented a device that could easily encrypt sensitive communications. He offered it to the German Navy & Foreign Office, but they politely declined. They already had codes, which, they claimed, were perfectly adequate. (They weren't, because the British were reading them). The war ended quickly and Germany no longer required codes. In 1923 Scherbius and Ritter established a new company, Chiffriermaschinen Akten-Gesellschaft and started selling an improved version to the banks.

A few banks liked the idea that they could send messages that no one could see. Scherbius also sold enough machines to sustain the company's existence. New machines were made and the original model, a massive machine that weighed over 100 lbs, was refined to be less than a quarter of its weight and compact enough to be carried in an elegant wooden case. Several hundred were exported. Scherbius ran into the streets without looking and was eventually run over by an animal. 1933 saw the Nazis take power and begin a secretive, huge rearmament drive. Chiffriermaschinen Akten-Gesellschaft abruptly stopped trading publically, and the machines disappeared off the market. [9] A new factory was soon to be open, and it was producing thousands of even more sophisticated machines. Scherbius named his machine Enigma. He also created commercial versions A through D. In 1928, the Enigma G, the last Scherbius design was adopted by pre-Nazi Germany. These machines proved difficult but not impossible to defeat. This new version was reserved for German military usage only. It was named the Enigma-I.

The Enigma-I or Service Enigma came in a case measuring eleven inches by six inches and just over one foot in length. The top of the case revealed a simple 26-key typewriter-style keyboard using the German QWERTZ layout. A matching panel of 26 lamp labels was above it. The top casing was adorned with three slots. Each slot had the notched edge from a wheel projecting through it. The plugboard contained 26 numbered double sockets. These can be joined together by using short plug-tipped wires. The case was made out of varnished, brass fittings with the machine's body in black-painted metal. The lid held spare plugboard cables as well as paper notices containing instructions about proper use and security. The machine's steel body contained a battery of 4.5 volts and an electromechanical circuit of fiendish complexity.

The basic principle of secret codes is that the messages' actual letters - also known as cleartext alphabet – are swapped out for other symbols in a cyphertext Alpha. The vast majority of children are familiar with simple codes. A steppingcode is a familiar one; the cyphertext letter is simply the cleartext, but "stepped up" to certain places. It would look like this when you take six steps:

ABCDEFGHIJKLMNOPQRSTUVWXYZ

GHIJKLMNOPQRSTUVWXYZABCDEF

Another common version of the keyword code is the keyword-code. Here, a keyword without repeated letters is chosen to be the starting point for the cyphertext. It would look as follows if the keyword selected was cypher.

ABCDEFGHIJKLMNOPQRSTUVWXYZ

CYPHERABDFGIJKLMNOQSTUVWXZ

To encode a message you just need to match each cleartext letter with the corresponding cyphertext letter. The message is encoded by the first code.

This is an encyphered phrase

Then it would be:

ZNOY OY GT KTIVNKXKJ SKMMGMK

To make it easier to understand individual words and learn some substitutions, it is a smart idea to break down the message in "words", which can be as long as five characters.

ZNOYO YGTKTIVNKX MGMK

A simple substitution code cypher can prevent casual attackers readable a message. It is vulnerable and could be subject to attack by cryptanalysts - codebreakers. It is monoalphabetic which means the same substitution is used to send the entire message. Letters do not appear in the same frequency. Some letters have a higher frequency than others. E is the most common English letter. K would be guessed by cryptanalysts as the equivalent of E. You can also do the same thing with the letters of other alphabets, though with less accuracy as you work your way down the list. But for messages over 100 characters, it's almost always possible to get half of them that way. It's possible for intelligence analysts, at that point, to guess the remainder. This weakness affects all monoalphabetic Cyphers.

Next is to use the polyalphabetic (or multi-alphabetic) cypher. This uses multiple alphabets throughout the message. A different alphabet is used for each character to make it more secure. Concentric disks were used to encode cleartext and cyphertext alphabets. This first example was discovered in 1467. The first character was encyphered. After that, the cyphertext device was moved one letter forward and the second character encoded. This was repeated for each letter. Each substitution was unique, and frequency analysis could no longer be used. The problem was that both the sender AND the receiver needed identical disks sets. Enemies could then get the disk and attack the Cypher. They wouldn't know which start position to use. However, 26 attempts would suffice for them to be successful and they'd be able then to read messages.

Over the next century more complex polyalphabetic Cyphers were made, culminating with the Vigenere Sypher (1586). This grid used 26 alphabets, each one of which was stepped by one position. These were then used according to a keyword. It was thought to have been indestructible even during the American Civil War. Confederate Army also used it. Charles Babbage (the English computer pioneer) had in fact quietly broken it back in 1846. The USA was able break the Confederate codes frequently because the keywords are easily guessed. But Babbage is a skilled mathematician and had managed a true, cryptanalytical attack. He identified a weakness in the key that was repeated at a predetermined interval. Repeated words or even parts of words could be enchaded at the same point in alphabet sequence patterns.

The polyalphabetic cyphers proved to be far more secure then monoalphabetic. However, the key repeat intervals must not exceed a very long time so they are still possible to be broken. The problem was that long keys were difficult to create and used by hand. Scherbius, along with the German Army, had created a machine capable of creating an almost infinite number polyalphabetic alphabetic alphabets. It had a repeat interval that was really amazing.

The keyboard is what makes the Enigma machine tick. The keys for each letter in the alphabet are identical to the keys found on an old-fashioned stylewriter. The keys can be difficult to push. Because a key is not only used to flick up a lightweight metal arm, but also a stiff one that can be pushed. It actually does two important things. It first moves a link between the rotors and the back of case. It also closes a switch, activating an electric circuit for the letter selected. The current runs through the machine and finally reaches one the 26 small letters lamps.

The exact configuration of the machine will determine which lamp it illuminates. The lamp is lit when the operator or an assistant notes the letter, then the assistant types the next letter. It may look simple from the outside but it's not. With every press of a key, the machine performs nine different substitutions.

THE STECKERBRETT

The flow of current from a battery first reaches the plugboard in the machine's front when the key is pressed. Steckerbrett was always the German name of this device. It has 26 sockets. There is one for each letter in the alphabet. Each socket has a different size hole. These can be connected together using short cables.

Pressing E will send current to the socket marked E. The socket could be connected with any other letter or no at all. If the socket's sprung contact is not energized, then the current will go on as E. The machine came standard with 12 cables, 10 for normal use and 2 spares.

Strangely, with 11 pairs of sockets connected, there is the greatest number of ways to set it up. Less sockets will give you fewer combinations.

Germans used ten sockets because it was easier. This gave three quarters as many alphabets as eleven. However, the number of letters was still well over 150 millions. It is possible to break it using letter frequency analyses, but once it was established the same substitution would have been used for each letter.

THE ROTORS

The current travels from the Steckerbrett onwards to the Eintrittwalz (entry rotor). This is a rigid disk with 26 contacts. Each of these contacts is connected to an socket on the board. It is surrounded by three rotors. Each of them looks similar to a wheel with a notched and extended edge. There are 26 contacts located on either side of the wheel. These contacts are wired together in pairs. The A contacts on the right and left of the wheel don't connect to each other; they are connected to one another.

The original machine came equipped with three rotors. Each of them could be installed in any location. Each machine was equipped with an identical set. Rotors were marked with Roman numerals, I, II, or III. The A contact of rotor 1 is wired on the right to E; the B contact on the left is wired on K, C, and M. The first three pairs in rotor 2 are A, B, J and C-D. Each rotor would substitute a letter and wire them together.

However, the outer rings can be a problem. Each ring comes with a notch on its edge. The ring can be rotated about the rotor up to 26 positions. The numbers and letters of the rings can be clearly seen through the three small windows. However, it is possible to still set the machine up in 26 other ways if the letter is visible. With six possible orders of rotors, that means another 105.456 possible alphabets.

THE REFLECTOR

After the current has passed all three rotors the reflector will be activated. This is another fixed-wheel, with 26 contacts on one end. These are wired together in pairs. This means that currents from one contact go out through the other. There were two reflectors. Each one had a different wiring. This doubled how many alphabets could be created by the Steckerbrett.

After leaving the reflector, the current travels back through them again and makes three more substitutions. Because the current is entering the row of rotors from a different contact, it takes a completely new path through them before reaching a contact on the Eintrittswalz. From there, it passes through the steckers (the ninth and last substitution) before coming back out at a contact on the Eintrittswalz. When the key is pressed, the circuit goes off and the lamp is turned off. However, the path of the next letter through the machine will be different.

The last and most difficult refinement of Enigma is the system connecting the keyboard to rotors. A key presses a small steel lever that moves against the notched edge at the first rotor. The pawl rotates the rotor for one twenty-sixth. Once it stops, the circuit closes, and the lamp lights up. When he types the next letter, he sees that the rotor is moving again. As the circuit closes, six substitutions performed by the rotors will have changed. If the machine was set up in a particular way, the operator could press and hold E. The R lamp would then light up. If the operator presses E once more, the R lamp would light up. If the message takes too long, a stud from the second rotor flips the third.

Since the cypher can only do letter frequency analysis, repeat interval analysis is not possible. The intervals are so vast that repeat interval analysis also won't work. The machine can be set up in a number of different ways, with ten letter pairings steckered and three rotors.

British cryptanalysts were faced by an apparently impossible task. Each Enigma message letter was encrypted with a different alphabet. Another German signaler set up an Enigma machine in exactly the same way that the one that had encyphered their message. Then, it was easy to convert the plaintext back into text. The number of alphabets available was astounding, even though no one knew how to set it all up. In fact, there were numerous.

107,458,491,300,000,000,000,000

Many of them. With such an enormous number, the intelligence officers decided to do only the sensible thing. They asked a mathematician.

Chapter 6: The Fighting Of The Odds

GC&CS were not actually the first ones to ask a mathematician for a review of Scherbius's terrifying invention. The Polish Army was extremely worried about Hitler. Hitler was loudly threatening their country with seizing the areas that once belonged to Germany. They had been carefully studying Enigma since a long time. They began to hack the code as early as the 1920s, long before the Nazis took power. Three mathematicians of Poznan University joined Polish Cypher Bureau to tackle Enigma on September 1, 1932. Marian Rejewski Henryk Zigalski and Jerzy Rotiecki were their names.

French military intelligence learned of the Polish project in 1932. Two stolen German military documents were passed along with two Enigma keysheets. These sheets, just like the Enigma machine itself were key to Enigma's power. Key settings collectively comprised the key settings for the rotor, ring and letter order. Each machine on a radionet had to be set up using the same key settings in order for it to work. Every station received key sheets to help them do that. Each sheet contained the key settings needed to be used every single day for a period of one month.

Like other governments, they had purchased Enigmas in commercial quantities from Scherbius as early as the 1920s. They understood how the contacts in the reflectors or rotors were paired. Although they knew the wires were different in new military machines, they didn't know how. All of that changed when the French provided material. Rejewski made some remarkable calculations that allowed him to use key sheets as well as encyphered messages in order to identify the wiring of each reflector and military wheel. He was able build replicas. However, it didn't help him crack the code. He didn't have the key setting to decode a message. Instead, he had the task of setting up the machine, typing the first characters, and seeing if it produced readable German text. When this failed, he had to reset the machine to a different setting and try again until clear text was produced. That could mean trying a substantial fraction of all the machine's possible settings - and there were 107,458,491,300,000,000,000,000 of them.

Enigma is a very old system. One of its flaws is that it cannot encrypt letters as they are. Any lamp could light up if E is typed on the keyboard.

This is a normal problem when using rotors that have a reflector. However, this is not a major issue. Enigma, when used properly, was very secure indeed. In fact, it is still very secure. Modern Enigma I machines have a key strength equal to 76-bit encryption. A national security agency could use supercomputers and brute force to crack the code. Although multiple Cray Cray YMPs are working on the code, it can take up to three or four days. The U-Boat Enigma M4 had 84-bit encryption. The NSA might take a few years to crack that. Although it's possible to break Enigma with brute force, it's a difficult task today. In 1939, this was impossible. Enigma enthusiasts manage to sometimes break original wartime messages on their home computers in just a few hours. [10] How?

The answer is straightforward. They don't just use brute force, but use a range of techniques to reduce the possibilities. That's also what the Poles and later, the British did. Mathematics was not enough. Breaking Enigma required both math and cunning.

The Polish trio stayed away from the machine for a while to focus on understanding how it was operated. Slowly, the hints began to pile up. German operators were inexperienced and many operating instructions contained errors. Every day, three letters were used to determine the start position of rotors. When the machine was set-up, the letters appeared in the three window. The sender would then choose the three new letters, encrypt them on the computer, and then send them. Finally, the machine would be reset to those letters. The receiver would decrypt these letters, then put them on his machine and decode their message. The Germans made a terrible mistake. To avoid any errors caused by poor radio reception, the Germans ordered that this encrypted wheel starting position be sent twice. The Enigma message had six letters. However, they were the same letters. The Poles discovered that the first, fourth and fifth letters of an Enigma message, as well as the second and fifth, third, and sixth letters, were all different in cyphertext. However, plaintext revealed that they were the same letter.

This wasn't the reflector bug, although it is theoretically a problem. However, it was far less serious than it seems. This was a significant weakness. They were familiar with the wiring and could begin to reconstruct the key setting. There were hundreds of thousands more possibilities than before, but it was small enough that a competent mathematician could work with it. Rejewski compiled a card list of patterns identified in six-letter groups. This index could help him determine which rotors were in use and in what order. To speed up the process, he designed a machine. He could quickly identify the day's rotor orders in just fifteen minutes. While he still wasn't able to determine the stecker connections nor the ring settings of his rotors, that didn't really matter. Enigma was reduced down to a monoalphabetic, complex cypher with the key element of the continually stepping rotors neutralized. Frequency analysis could break this.

He found himself suddenly shut down in November 1937. It was the first sign he had of a problem, which would continue to haunt him until the end. Enigma was a moving target. Germans always had new ideas for making it even more secure. Modularity made it easy for them. Making additional components was the easiest option, and they did just that. The reflector was the only thing that came with every machine. The second, which was wired differently, was issued.

Also, the key setting was changed to indicate which one was to go to use that day. Rejewski, who had guessed the cause of the problem, began creating a new index to match the reflector. This took almost a full year. The problem was not over.

Actually, there were already problems. The Kriegsmarine, Germany's Navy, was notorious for having the most strict Enigma use procedures. Their traffic was impossible to read for extended periods. They stopped encoding simple texts and switched to a book-based code system in May 1937. Standard formats were designed for all types and types of messages. They could send contact reports, weather updates or changes to course. These formats were filled using four-number groups of code numbers that each represented a word or phrase. "Enemy is sight" was not written as "Feind-in-sitt"; it was now 0292. [11] These numbers can be converted to letters with a simple substitutioncode, then encoded on Enigma. Even if the key settings of the replica machine were correct, even a cryptanalyst wouldn't know if they had broken the code.

The darkening of signals for the Army, Air Force and Navy also occurred in May 1938. Germans had changed this procedure. Operators used a new Grundstellung to send each message. This was not a serious problem. Many operators were lazy, choosing the same letters for every message. Cilli was a famous operator who had a girlfriend. He always set his machine on CIL. Poles found it easier to make such mistakes. Henryk Zigalski had already invented a new tool.

Sometimes, approximately 12 percent, of all messages, one of six characters in the vital first six characters will contain the same letter twice. Zygalski named this "Female" because women have a double version of the X that men have. If the first six letters were KXLQXM and the fifth letter was plaintext, then XX would be the 2nd & 5th letters. Because the Poles knew the rotor- and reflector wiring, they had an additional way in. He created 26 large sheets with letters marked and punched with patterns of holes. Each sheet represented a possible position to start the first rotor. They simulated the settings for the machine by being arranged in stacks and then moved in a carefully planned pattern. At first, there would be many letters visible through the holes of the top sheet. Zygalski could make the right predictions and the number would drop until there was only one. That would mark the start position for the first rotation. Rejewski's catalog only records the start positions that can produce females. Therefore, the order of the rotors could be deduced. The frequency analysis then revealed the steckering.

This was not a problem. It was necessary to have a different stack for each of six possible rotor orders. With limited resources, the team needed to make these sheets. With a razor blade, this meant that the sheets needed to be printed, and the holes had to be cut. Zygalski could only complete two sets, by mid-December 1938. Then disaster struck.

The Germans unveiled two new rotors, IV, and V, on December 15. Six rotor orders could now be 60. That meant 60 sheets would be required. Zygalski had been working for weeks on his sheets and had accomplished only a third. It was clear that the task was impossible now. The Poles found themselves disillusioned and decided to try Rejewski's new plan. Rejewski decided that since the German computer cypher was created using a machine, maybe it could also be broken. He devised six triple drums to mimic an Enigma-rotor stack. It relied on females, much like the Zygalski papers, to find the key setting. The Zygalskis sheets required ten males, while the new machine needed only three. Plugs were used to detect the females. Once the machine was switched on, each drum tested one order of rotors before it could make a circuit. The spinning drums would be stopped by electromagnets. The machine had 17576 options and could test them all within a matter of hours. It was known as the bomba-kryptologiczna (the "cryptologic Bomb") by Rejewski. This machine was a great success.

The new rotors arrived.

Rejewski could wire the new rotors for the SS in just a few weeks. However, the SD, an intelligence agency of SS hadn't updated their procedures and still used a single Grundstellung for every day's message. However, it wasn't very useful as there was an increase in the number and possibilities of settings by a factor 10. Ten bombas were required to test all 60 possible order rotors. The Poles set about building them but had completed only four by July 1939. Politically, the situation was quickly deteriorating. In just weeks, war with Germany was almost certain. They then decided to ask for assistance.

Jusqu'à présent, the British and French allies of Poland knew about Enigma. They didn't know that Enigma was broken. The Poles called in secret and requested that the British and French leading cryptanalysts attend a conference. Alfred Dillwyn Knox was the leader for the British delegation. Knox, an irritable genius, had previously worked as a code breaker at Naval Intelligence. British cryptanalysts called Knox a legend. This was partly because he had helped to break the "Zimmerman Telegram," revealing German treachery. The revelations brought the USA in the war in 1917. Knox had met the Poles already in January 1939. But they hadn't disclosed their successes. They had already been impressed by Knox's Enigma knowledge, so they invited him along to their conference. Knox agreed to go to Warsaw on 27 July. Knox carried a paper slip rule he developed that could break any Enigma model. It could also be used by the Spanish fascists. He also took Alan Turing.

Turing was amazed by the work that the three young Poles had done, possibly because he was a mathematician and Knox was an expert on ancient Egyptian scrolls. He had studied some aspects of Enigma and passed that knowledge along to the Poles. He also had a lot to do from them and soaked it all up. Their lack of resources was what Turing was less impressed with. Turing had been working as a part-time worker for GC&CS starting in September 1938. Turing was well aware that the urgency of the situation. He was shocked to learn that Zygalski's sheets had been made by hand, and it was so slow and inefficient. The formula for the sheets, which was part of the package that the Poles had given to Knox at the end of the conference, was found in his luggage. Turing quickly reacted when he got back from England. One printer was able to perforate sheets of paper. This was sworn to secret. So sixty sheets were run and a printing machine fitted with a stamper and perforator fitted on each one. Turing was able achieve what Zygalski had struggled to do for months. The heavy bundle of sheets didn't make it to Warsaw. First, it was taken to a shabby mansion in an English small town.

Chapter 7: Bletchley Poark

Knox was an officer in Naval Intelligence, the First World War. Their headquarters were in London's Admiralty Building. It was there that they worked in Room 40, the famous office. The war would be different though, it was evident. In 1937, Guernica was bombed in Spain. This showed that the Nazis could have a large bomber force and would not hesitate using it against towns and cities. London's Whitehall district with its government and military offices would be a obvious target. If Encryptanalysis were to be a powerful weapon against the Reich's military power, it was essential that codebreakers be safe. Therefore, a new location needed to search. There was also the suspicion that Enigma would generate more traffic than could be handled by a handful of people with pencils in their hands, sitting in large offices. In 1938, a small group began looking for a country house they could discreetly purchase. Soon, however, Bletchley became the center of attention.

Bletchley lies fifty miles north from London. Now it is part of the post-War New Town of Milton Keynes. Before it was abruptly removed from neighborhood status by the planners of 1967, it had existed at least since the 12thcentury. It was a small village when it was established in 1845. But, the London and North West Railway opened the year that gave it a boost of importance. Soon, the station became a hub for four major railway lines and hundreds of trains each day. Bletchley saw a boom in Victorian construction, which helped it expand. The town was constructed on heavy clay soil. It soon became an industrial hub for bricks. Today, the area is home to artificial lakes created from the old clay mines. Bletchley in 1938 was a typical small town. It was dominated primarily by the chimneys and brickworks kilns. It was also coated with light soot from LNWR-line trains.

Near the southeast corner Bletchley is a large house. It's located 400 yards from Bletchley Station and the rail yards. A large house has stood on this spot for almost a thousand years. It is situated in the middle of 580 acres of farmland and meadows. Nearly everyone agrees with the fact that this house was built back in 1883. The house, which is a mixture of local red brick and honey-colored limestone, has all of the splendor of a Victorian mansion without any of the elegance. It had been home to a single resident since 1937. The new owner was planning to demolish and develop the area for housing. A Captain Faulkner of Naval Intelligence was actually the head of the syndicate which bought the estate. Admiral Sir Hugh Sinclair had been his boss before and was no longer interested in waiting for the government. Faulkner, who had bid at an auction for the house, paid for the purchase and handed it over to the codebreakers. [12] Sinclair fought against the government to get back his money, but GC&CS came in.

Bletchley residents had expected to see the bulldozers arrive at their house to flatten it. Instead, the gate was reopened and Captain Ridley's shooting party started roaming the grounds. They were actually taking a careful survey of the property to see how many people they could hold and how large it could be expanded into a codebreaking operation. Soon, Post Office technicians arrived to discreetly install new telephone lines connecting the old house to London.

The chance of avoiding war had ended by August 1939. Bletchley Park became the official home to GC&CS. People began arriving in Bletchley. Germany invaded Poland, September 1, prompting Neville Chamberlain's fateful ultimatum for Hitler: withdraw or otherwise. Hitler, who had an understandable low opinion about the western Allies' resolve - afterall, they'd done absolutely nothing when he'd overthrown the Rhineland. Austria, Sudetenland, and the rest of Czechoslovakia. - dismissed it airily as a joke. It wasn't just a bluff this time. Chamberlain understood how dangerous Hitler was and was now able to recognize that Hitler's threat was actually real. On September 3, German troops were still pushing into Poland, brutally wiping out any resistance. Chamberlain then announced that Britain was now at the war with Germany. Similar declarations from France and the British Empire countries followed. Bletchley's staff began arriving on the site the next morning, and within hours "Station X" had become operational.

Alistair Denniston, Royal Navy Commandant, ran Station X. Denniston, who had worked in Room 40 with Knox during World War One, was now in charge of Britain's whole cryptanalysis effort.

Knox was responsible in the attack on Enigma. Turing and Gordon Welchman from Cambridge arrived on September 4th to aid him. They had all the Polish tools in their possession, including one Rejewski's replica Enigmas. But progress was slow, and messages were not broken for months. The USSR invaded Poland from east and the Polish Cypher Bureau suddenly found their Warsaw headquarters in immediate danger. They fled south through Romania – the two countries shared an border at the time. Rozycki joined the PC Bruno signal intercept station in Paris as soon as Zygalski was released. PC Bruno quickly established direct telegraph cables to Bletchley Park. These two stations worked closely together for nine months. Ironically the message traffic was secure by the replica Enigmas. Although they had Turing at one end and Rejewski on the other end, their encryption procedures didn't have the same errors as those of the Germans.

Turing and Knox were both worried that the Poles had succeeded in breaking into the German Enigma code system. All Polish methods had one weakness: Germans sending the message key twice. Germans might change their ways at any time. It was important to find a robust way to crack the code.

The Poles had taken a look at the Enigma's reflector and recognized that it was not a fatal flaw. However, it could still be exploited in certain situations. The message key vulnerability was the best choice, as it was less difficult. Turing & Welchman looked again. Normally, the fact of the machine not being able to decipher any message meant little. But, if the cryptanalyst was able to guess or know part of the plaintext, then things did change. Any position where the letters of the plaintext were not identical could be eliminated if it could be easily slid along the cyphertext line. This would result in a significantly smaller number possible positions where plaintext/cyphertext might be identical.

By this time the Enigma had 1,074,584,913,000,000,000,000,000 possible key settings, but starting with the same piece of cyphertext they would all create different cyphertexts. The British could identify the key setting that could have produced the message by using part of the message. From there, they could build their own machine and decode it all. A "crib" was a term that refers to a piece of plaintext known or guessed by Bletchley Park.

The problem was there. Bletchley might have had a crib or intercepted a message. Only one key setting could have produced the one you were looking for. But which one? There were 1,074,584,913,000,000,000,000,000 possibilities, after all. There was only one way to quickly review all the possibilities. Turing still had his Zygalski sheets in full, but they were evidently too slow. Turing thought back to July's bomba Rejewski. Despite its limitations, the device appealed to Rejewski because of his personal interest in computing. The technology to create one was still unknown. A Turing machine could, however, be programmed to solve any problem. It was possible to create a machine that solved a single problem.

Turing had been only a few days at Bletchley before he began to sketch the design. He wanted to avoid relying on the repeated message key as the bomba's main weakness and create something that could easily attack messages with a crib. He also wanted it faster. The bomba was capable of breaking the key in only a few hours when there were three rotors. However, that time became almost a full day when there were now five. His solution was revolutionary. Once the concept was finished, it was necessary to produce a real design. Turing wasn't an engineer but a mathematician.

They were once again successful. Someone remembered that British Tabulating Machine Company was located in Letchworth 20 miles away. BTM was initially established to sell electromechanical adding machines. These machines were imported first by the US Tabulating Machine Company (which later became IBM in 1924) before being renamed to BTM. BTM chief engineer Harold Keen (or Doc) was drawn in to make Turing's sketches a reality.

Rejewski's bomba with six drums was relatively small and could be easily sat on a dining table. Turing's bombe, however, was enormous. It was seven feet across, two feet deep, and six and a bit feet high. It weighed over one ton and contained 111 drums. Each scrambler resembled an Enigma Machine and the drums themselves were color-coded in order to identify which Enigma Rotor they were imitating. They could be mounted on any of the three axles. Simulated reflectors could be found at each end. There were 26-way cables running back to the rear, making it easy to reconfigure the machine quickly. Cribs became "menus" when they were connected to the enormous machine using a plugboard. The machine could then test not only rotor orders, mais also stecker connections. The bombe used an electrical motor and top drums that were fast enough to match the Enigma right rotor's speed of 50.4 rpm. With 26 combinations being checked every revolution of a drum, each scrambler was able to test 22 key settings every second. [13] The bombe could scan 792 keys per second; 47.520 within a minute; and almost six millions in the time it took Rejewski's machine 175,26 to check.

It was still way too slow.

Victory, the park's first bombe was delivered on March 18, 1941. Turing & Keen had been working on improvements to the bomber before it arrived. It would operate at 120 rpm and produce 1,872 keys per sec. The problem was not the only one. Like its Polish counterparts, the bombe tested every key by trying to run an electricity current through the scrambler. The scrambler whirred if there wasn't a circuit. A circuit would cause the machine to stop, and the operator would then read the solution on the indicator drums. A cryptanalyst then checked each solution for logical contradictions. If no nonsense emerged, the bombe was re-activated. If German text emerged the key was destroyed. The problem with the bombe was that it didn't have a very long crib, up to 150 letters, so it made a lot of false starts. Bletchley struggled to find the right resources for testing these.

Gordon Welchman then suggested an improvement. He created an attachment that would attach to the bombe. It used the fact that the stecker connections were symmetrical. A was steckered at B and B was steckered at A. This allowed for a reduction in false stops. The diagonal board, or the diagonal device, dramatically reduced the required crib size. The cryptanalysts desired cribs that had at least twelve letters. However, if they needed to, they could run a bombe with eight letters.

Turing had visited CP Bruno with the Poles during the building of the first bombe by BTM in January 1940. He presented the Zygalski sheets to them he'd made last year, and discussed their progress. Zygalski (with Rejewski) achieved the first Enigma code break since October 1939. CP Bruno managed to crack around 17 percent of Enigma codes cracked by the Allies over the period of the 1940s. It was a remarkable performance given their limited resources. Turing, however, could see the writing at the wall. Their ideas were brilliant but not lasting.

On May 10, 1940 the Germans launched an offensive through Holland. Belgium. Luxembourg to try and outflank the French borders defenses. Because just before the Wehrmacht began to roll, the Wehrmacht had its message traffic go dark. Enigma breaks stopped abruptly. Turing was wrong. The Germans changed their message key procedures and all Polish techniques suddenly became ineffective. It was time that the bombe was actually spun up.

Chapter 8: Blitzkrieg

The British Expeditionary Force (French Army) and the British Army had expected an attack and were well aware of the possibility that German forces would come through Belgium. There was an interesting blind spot in American and British military thinking about Belgium's Ardennes region, which is hilly and densely wooded. The terrain was not suitable for large-scale operations, even though the Germans had successfully done so in 1914, 1870, and 1917. They did it again, in 1940. [2] France's defences believed that if they did arrive this way, the Belgian Army would provide them with several weeks to prepare strong defenses for the advance.

They were horribly wrong. Rommel and Guderian were the hard-charging Panzer generals Rommel (and Guderian), who led the German forces into Belgium on May 10. They had overcome every resistance by May 14th, and major fighting was underway on French soil. Just three weeks later, the panzers headed towards Paris. PC Bruno was shut down and staff dispersed as the Wehrmacht ended its existence. Rejewski (Zygalski) and Zygalski fled to France, along with many French cryptoanalysts. Finally they managed to make their way towards neutral Spain and then caught ships to Britain. They were however damaged goods. None of them could trust because they had been in Vichy France. Two Poles joined the Free Polish Army, where they worked to crack hand-cyphered SS/SD code codes. They were never allowed near Bletchley. The Polish contribution in the war against Enigma was complete. The British cryptanalysts went it alone.

They were expecting it, but they were as prepared as they could be. Turing had accomplished a remarkable feat, eliminating many key settings for each daily traffic. He discovered that while each message was sent at a different beginning position, sometimes the message's rotors would change to the previous start position. To identify this, he designed a system for punching received messages into long-format index cards. The repeated sequences were found by overlaying the cards on an illuminated table. The cards measured several yards and were named "Banburies", after the town from which they were made. Turing's many oddities included his tendency to use German word endings. Banburismus was born from this habit. It allowed the bombe to perform faster.

In August 1940, another bombe was finished. Welchman had his diagonal board installed. The original bombe was returned to factory to have the board fit. The timing was perfect as the Battle of Britain was still raging. At the time, the Germans tried bombing first London and then the Royal Air Force. Bletchley made its first break into German Air Force communications in May. By August, Bletchley was reading the messages regularly. The Park's Air Intelligence Office expected the daily key to be broken at breakfast. British pilots knew the targets and could then position their fighters to meet them. Bletchley also gathered valuable information about Germany's air force strength. Churchill's resistance was encouraged by the fact that Hitler didn't have as few bombers as feared.

Bletchley had another goal that year. Britain had feared invading Germany since June's withdrawal from France. Wehrmacht workers had been preparing for an invasion by constructing barges along the Channel ports. The planned invasion was delayed repeatedly after the summer's brutal raids on the Channel failed to win air superiority, much less over south England. In September, Hitler was informed by bombings. Dutch airfields were the first to be notified that air transport units had been ordered to cease preparations for a landing and de-equip their equipment. This was quickly understood by the intelligence team. The invasion was stopped at least through 1941. In reality, this plan would never be revived. By early next year, the attention of the fickle dictator had shifted east to Russia's graveyard of his Thousand Year Reich.

The end to the invasion threat didn't mean that the war would cease, however. Air raids continued, with cities and ports being hammered every night. Savage battles were fought by the air forces and naval units of both sides to try and take over the Channel, and North Sea. The war in North Africa heated up. In the Atlantic, Britain was facing a new campaign that would see it closer to defeat than ever before.

Chapter 9: The Gray Wolves

Treaty of Versailles which ended the First World War had severely limited Germany's navy. This included a ban on the construction of submarines. A Dutch secret submarine design office was set-up, and Hitler's government had already begun to build advanced designs. The Nazi dictator quickly began finding ways around the restrictions of treaty, including building limited numbers of U-Boats to "research"/"training" purposes. Soon, however, he was freely flouting them. The Kriegsmarine owned a fleet 65 U.Boats, which grew rapidly at the beginning of the war.

It was unsafe for U-Boats early in war to even reach the Atlantic. The Royal Navy still controlled the English Channel (and North Sea) and many submarines were lost as they tried breaking through. The fall of France however changed everything. Large, bomb-proof U.Boat pens were constructed around the Bay of Biscay. From these bases, boats could sail directly to the open ocean. They could travel further west to patrol the Atlantic longer and can also range further in the Atlantic as they are 450miles further west. Britain is heavily dependent on US shipments of fuel, food, raw materials and other supplies. This could have disastrous consequences. Royal Navy's antisubmarine boats were fitted with ASDIC, which is the best sonar in the world. However, it could only detect submarines within 200 yards. It was great at finding and attacking U-Boats previously identified visually or by radar. But it didn't have the range necessary to search 41,000,000 miles of ocean for quiet, small boats. Churchill was optimistic that Bletchley Park could find the Uboats by intercepting them and reading their messages. The problem was that the Kriegsmarine had extremely secure key settings, making it impossible to read those messages.

Turing was already researching the Naval Enigma. He usually stated that "No-one else was going to do anything about it and it was my right to have it for myself."[14] By using work done by the Poles, Turing was able find the complex, but still very simple, message key procedures. Although the standard naval machine was called the M3, it was almost identical to the Enigma-I. The only difference was that the rotor rings had numbers instead of letters and that the wires were wired in the same manner. It wasn't long until he made an astonishing discovery. The Poles were kept out of German traffic by two more rotors. Turing soon discovered that the Kriegsmarine had issued additional three rotors, numbered VI-VII and VIII. This increased the possible rotor orders from 60 to 336 and the possible key settings to 6,017,675,512,800,000,000,000,000.

That could have markedly changed the course of war and ended the battle for the Naval Enigma. But the situation was subtlety different. Enigma machine were held at regimental or division headquarters as well on Luftwaffe bases. Given the German advance everywhere, it was unlikely that they would be captured. Britain was still dominant at sea. The Royal Navy ruled the world until late 1943 when the US Navy surpassed it. German ships had to be careful when they set sail from the coast. Many of them weren't able to get away with this, so the RN were given strict instructions to board German shipping whenever possible and steal cryptographic material. These recoveries were called "pinches" in Bletchley's words and were very helpful. Pinches could include people as well material. One captured radio operator confirmed the fact that numbers could now be written as text. Hut 8 Turing's Naval Enigma unit, an analysis of plaintext German naval messages found that more 90% of them had the number 1, written EINS. They developed a database detailing how EINS was deciphered at every M3 Enigma rotor setting - all 105.456 of them. After that, they began to use a BTM machine to search for these settings every time they received a naval message. Sometimes the steckering concealed it, but occasionally E, N, S and I would match. False matches did occur, but about one in four matches ended up being true. Hut8 knew the rotor setting, ring position, and order of the match. Only the steckering needed to be broken.

Banburismus was also helpful. One simple substitution code, based off a bigram-table table, was used to conceal the Navy message keys. Turing then slowly rebuilt it using lots of calculations and clues. Banburismus could reduce 336 possible order rotors down to 18, simplifying bombe meals by a factor twenty when the table was rebuilt.

Unknown wiring was the problem. U-33 got a surprise when HMS Gleaner (patrol ship) laid mines near the Scottish coast. For several hours she hammered on the submarine with depth charge and finally succeeded in forcing her to surface. Although the boat's crew had prepared to abandon her, they set self-destructive charges on the submarine and then threatened to destroy it. But the officers were afraid that the British could save the Enigma. There was not enough time to take the machine out of the radio desk, so the precious rotors had to be lifted and distributed to three crewmen. Two of them did. Friedrich Kumpf, however, failed to do so. He was almost dead from hypothermia and panicking so he was taken aboard Gleaner and brought below to warmth up. He only began to feel better and remembered the rotors. Kumpf had his pants hanging out to dry. The pockets were not empty. The British had three of these rotors including VI and VIII. [15]

HMS Griffin captured a German armoured trawler. On April 26, the Enigma machine crossed the side before Griffin's marines could board her. But they managed to capture an instruction booklet and some decoded message. They managed to cut six days' worth traffic almost immediately.

These numbers and Turing's mathematical work made slow progress on the M3-code, but it was getting increasingly desperate out there. The U-Boot-Waffe described the period of June 1940 to March 1941 as the Happy Time. They could leave their boats unattended over most of the Atlantic and strike crucial supply convoys at will. U-Boats brought down 284,113 tonnage of shipping. It was a much smaller number, but it was still very serious: 195.825 ton. The numbers continued to rise, with 267.618 tons in august and 293,335 in septembrie. Britain owned 33% of the world's shipping cargo, but this large fleet couldn't keep up with its rapid growth. Bletchley must break into M3. Lieutenant Commander Ian Fleming, the creator of James Bond, devised a wild plan to capture a German boat patrolling with all its communications equipment intact. With a crew comprising disguised commandos and a crew of German bombers, he would intentionally crash the captured German aircraft in the Channel. The Germans sent an assault team to kill the crew and bring the boat back to England. While the plan was sound, Turing and Peter Twinn learned the terrible news. [16] U.Boats had lost 352,407 ton of shipping in October.

Then there was a brief pause. As the winter storms came to an end, the submarine threat was lessened. U-boats at sea were unable to find a convoy visually, making it much harder for them to avoid being attacked. These losses were slightly lower: 146.613 tons in November and 212.590 in Dec., but "only" 126,782 in January 1941. Turing anticipated that the number would rise as weather improved. But commandos raided the German base on Lofoten Island on March 4th. The attack resulted in the capture of Krebs' armed fishing boat and a set of complete naval rotors. They also found February's key setting sheet. Although it should have been destroyed, they discovered that these sheets had the days printed in reversed order. Thus, once a day ended, the key could be cut out of the sheet and burnt. In rare naval carelessness, the Krebs captain hadn't done that. Turing now knew he had everything he needed for his bigram table to be completed and the bombes upgraded to simulate rotor 8. The messages began to crack suddenly. Hut 8 had previously operated normal hours. But now, it switches to three shifts.

The Park job was hard and stressful but the station retained some of its pre-War university atmosphere. There were many talented musicians on staff and they often put on concerts in between shifts. The chess clubs thrived and many of their members - Turing being one of them - were highly skilled players. Eccentricity was also tolerated. Dilly Knox arrived sometimes at work in only his pajamas. One cryptanalyst was from the Japanese Section and used to swim naked on the ornamental water in front of the house. Turing was decently dressed but still managed to be more eccentric than many. He was affectionately known as "The Professor" for his unorthodox academic methods and his elaborate solutions to minor difficulties. Crockery was never in plentiful supply during World War II. Theft of mugs was a common problem. Turing was the first to secure his radiator in Hut 8 by chaining it to it and using a large padlock to lock it. To get to London meetings, he ran the 50-mile route to Whitehall. It was a remarkable demonstration of his physical endurance. For shorter trips around Park or to bombe stations, he bicycled. His bicycle was equally eccentric as Turing. After a certain length of time, the chain would come off the sprocket. Turing studied this problem and determined the interval. After that, he counted his pedal strokes during each cycle. The chain would come off, and

Turing would then retension the chain by turning the pedals around in reverse. Perhaps he was too busy to purchase a new chain. Maybe he saw some advantages to a bike that would not fall apart if another person tried to use. He would have severe hay fever attacks in early summer every year. He received a gas mask from Britain during the war. It blocked pollen well, but caused him alarm and then hilarity.

People laughed at the Prof and his silly quirks. Yet, work continued daily, 24 hours a day. Everyone understood that it was extremely important and dangerous.

HMS Aubretia, HMS Bulldog and HMS Broadway fought off U-110. They were aware that U-110 was damaged in an earlier attack. The entire crypto material was recovered by this boarding party. They also found the key settings for the month and codes books as well as backup hand-code sheets. [3] Submarine sank the next morning as the British were towing to Scapa Flow on the Orkney Island. However, its signal area had already been destroyed.

Germans wouldn't have believed that April's keys could have been stolen if the captured sailors had not written home to the Red Cross. German cryptanalysts had no doubt that Enigma could theoretically have been cracked, but they weren't convinced anyone would put in the effort. Their high command was convinced it was unbreakable. The British could have read April's traffic, they would think, but in May new key setting would be activated and the system will be secure again. They didn't know Turing was now equipped with four bombes, each capable of attacking the M3, as well as the fact that an increasing percentage of traffic was being hampered by the ever-spinning machines.

Within weeks, it was paying off. Shipping losses during the war were particularly severe in May and June. They were more than 300,000. The submarines were able to carry 94 209 tons in July and 80 311 tons in August. U-110 also captured the Critical Short Signal Book. This contained the U-Boats' code numbers instead of words, phrases. Despite the inaccessibility of the codes, they could create cribs with this information. Turing's Crib Room was born. By that time, Britain was covered with signal intercept points like Beaumanor, Chicksands and others. This station was also used during the Cold War by the USAF.

Now, it is the home of Britain's Intelligence Corps. These people didn't just hear the messages. They measured their bearings and used direction-finding tools to do so. If the same message was picked up by more than one station, the intersecting bearings would indicate the approximate location of the UBoat. The Crib Room could deduce that the UBoat was in close proximity to a ship and the message was a sighting reports. Bletchley was able to determine the contents of this message by looking at the ships the UBoat would be sighted. That would be their bed, which could then be checked and loaded onto the bombe. There was a good likelihood that the day's keys would be broken an hour later.

Bletchley was forced to be careful. They had intercepted the UBoats and knew exactly where they were. It would have taken little effort to send a bomber and destroyer to each location, inflicting heavy casualties on the U.Boat arm through a rapid series. But the victory would have ended quickly. Every intelligence organisation faces the dilemma how to use information. Overusing it too obviously can reveal the enemy what has been happening. However, if the

Germans were aware that Enigma was being compromised they could have rapidly increased their security. In fact, the British faced exactly the same problem as the German battleship Bismarck when they sought to capture it in May 1941. After fighting a series of battles with the Royal Navy, which saw it sink HMS Hood and damage a British battleship in battle, the ship was then allowed to slip into the Atlantic. She had sustained some injuries herself and the captain decided she should head for France. Turing's squad broke a battleship message on May 26, informing naval HQ of her turning towards Brest. Bismarck was in contact with the pursuing ships on the previous day. Germans could have assumed that she had lost her radio communication and were about to attack her again. Instead, a squadron PBY Catalina reconnaissance planes was sent from Northern Ireland to "search" the area and find the battleship. The crews of the planes believed the search to be genuine, but Park knew exactly what they would discover. [18] On May 26, Ensign Leonard B. Smith was a US Navy pilot, who'd unofficially delivered his PBY, then flew for RAF. Smith sighted Bismarck at 10:30am. Hours later, battleships closed in from every direction as torpedo bombarders began to strike. Bismarck was sunk early the following day by her crew, who believed to the last that the PBY had stopped them from fleeing.

While such elaborate deceptions were not necessary for the U-Boats war, there were still limits to what they could do without having to reveal their secret. They settled for diverting convoys towards U-Boats' concentrations and forming roving expedition groups to reinforce convoys that were severely threatened. It was enough. It was still difficult to lose, and they fluctuated for most of the following year. But the worst seemed over.

Chapter 10: Drumbeat Of Disaster

The Imperial Japanese Navy attacked Pearl Harbor in the US on December 7, 1941. They then abruptly pulled the USA into the war. Hitler declared war the following day, making the US Navy active in the Battle of the Atlantic. It was a very painful experience. Many US ships were working closely with Canadians as well as the British for several months. This helped to escort convoys into the western Atlantic. Crews had a thorough understanding of U-Boat threats. However, it didn't work for all their commanding officers. Admiral Ernest King who was in charge at home of US Navy ships refused to listen to the British. Instead of being split into convoys, US shipping continued to operate as before. King didn't place a blackout at the east coast because he didn't wish to hurt tourism. Instead, he kept lights on in towns and highways. The ships themselves diduse all the lights onboard, but that was no help. You could clearly see their silhouettes against the glowing shoreline, out at sea. The submarine commanders couldn't believe it.

Admiral Donitz was aware of the ease with which he was being hit and immediately threw all his long-range U boats at the east coast. Operation Drumbeat is the official name, but the men on the boats referred to it as the Second Happy Time.

It was a bloody massacre. Every night, U-Boats slowly slipped towards the US coast. Conning towers barely touched the surface. Soon, the silhouette of a ship would emerge. A U-Boat would launch a bomb if the ship is a tanker, a warship and a big freighter. Smaller ships were simply blasted to pieces with the deck gun. U-Boats pulled off the coast to get help from large Milchkuh supply vessels that had been following them across Atlantic. Turing's Hut 8 facilitated the passage of ships heading for Britain into tight, escorted convoys. Admiral King refused to provide daily submarine location reports for England and refused to build escortships. Any mention of the convoy system in his office was angrily rebutted. The slaughter didn't stop. Donitz, seeing all the Type IX long-range boats in US waters, pulled many Type VII submarines back to the convoy war, loaded them with fuel, rations, and sent them on their way to the east coast. December 1941 saw a loss of 120,070 Tons. In January 1942, that number increased to 327.357. By February, 476.451 tons had been added to the death toll. Although the USA was trying to supply Britain with its old destroyers, the Royal Navy decided to surrender brand-new Canadian escort vessels built in Canada. The problem wasn't with the ships. U-123 sank seven Long Island ships within a week in mid-January. There were 13 US Navy destroyers anchored in New York Harbor. King didn't direct them to sea. King did not act on the U-Boats in any way, even after half a millionne tons of shipping were lost in March. King's inaction came at an unfortunate time. The disaster that struck February 1st was unheard of, which he had not been paying attention to.

German radio traffic was broken into many nets using different key settings. Bletchley assigned them names. They called them first after colors. But, once they ran out they switched to animals or plants. The net for routine German navy traffic was called Dolphin. However messages to and form the UBoats went out via a separate wire. Germans could have their own names for the keys. They called it Triton after the messenger God of the seas. Bletchley's name was more descriptive. U-Boat net was named Shark.

Like Dolphin and several other naval nets Shark used M3 and Hut 8 at least two to three days per weeks. They supplied a constant stream of information throughout January 1942 to the Submarine Tracking Room at London. From there it was fed on to the convoys as well as - with increasing desperation and deafening - to Admiral King's ears. All was well, up to midnight Berlin-time on January 31, The remaining key sheets were burned at Donitz's headquarters near St Nazaire. The captain's sleeping quarters were taken out of the locked cabinet, and the sheets were placed on the desk in the radio shack near the Enigma. In each boat, a junior officer (or NCO) stripped the Enigma its cables & rotors and cleaned it with an oily paper before setting it all up for the new day. The plugs were snapped into the board, and the motors fell into the machine's guts. Each component was checked against its key setting to verify that it was in place. Finally, the operators closed all the covers and powered the machines up. There were four rotors.

Admiral Donitz disagreed with the German high command, who didn't believe Enigma could possibly be broken. In late 1941, Donitz had asked his naval cryptolgraphy team to study ways to increase the security and integrity of his beloved UBoats. They came up a simple yet clever solution. They began by using an M3 reflector as a starting point and developed a "thinner" reflector that was just half the size. Two versions were made, each with completely new wiring. They produced two "thinner" rotors. These rotors could not be interchanged with the I-VIII rotors, so they were given the names Beta and Gamma. The new reflector & rotor were the exact same width as the original reflector, and would fit in exactly the same place. The Enigma M4 then was born.

But, even though the new fourth rotation would never be turned in the same direction as its predecessor, that didn't matter. The Naval Signaling Procedures had strict limits for message lengths. Signals that exceeded 250 characters were subject to a new message-key selection. The Short Signal Book only allowed 22 characters. There were 52 possible key settings for the M3 with two new Rotors. Each of these could be turned to 26 positions. The new machine can be run as an MP3 - each new rotor could be coupled with one or more of the thin reflectors. In this position, it simulates an M3 reflector. UBoats are able to talk to surface ship's surface and use January's keys. Shark traffic was now 52x safer than Dolphin. Bletchley once more was blacked.

Although the bombes were able to be modified to work for M4 messages their runtime proved to be between fifty-a hundred and one hundred times longer then that of M3 intercepts. It meant that by the time an M4 message was read, it would be obsolete. They had to get Shark traffic read quickly enough to protect convoys. This took a lot of time. Turing understood that a more efficient bombe was necessary, but he couldn't understand how this could be achieved. After three long years of war, Britain had exhausted its resources. Both in terms of materials and manpower. He decided to have one built in the USA. But, while he was waiting for a permanent solution, he had to make a decision. He finally found one. It was found in U-110's short Signal Book.

U-Boats could send information to German naval airbases or surface ships. They didn't have the M4 machines. U-Boats used M3s to send information to Dolphin. More frequently, the U-Boats sent the information to Shark's St. Nazaire Headquarter. If

St. Nazaire was concerned that there might be others who need it, they would send it back in Dolphin. Turing entered the Crib Room and began to study the precise times on the message forms that were being delivered every day. Turing suspected that St. Nazaire would be repeating the message of the U-Boat by sending it a message. The signal from St. Nazaire was broken due to its top priority. Hut 8 would then encode the message using Short Signal Book. If they had been right, their message will match the UBoat original signal. It would be an excellent crib. They slowly began to break other messages, even though the M4 was more complicated. However, this wasn't enough.

In April, the US Navy instructed coastal shipping to sail in convoys if possible and to only move at daylight. Despite opposition from business leaders, there was no coastal blackout. U-85 was lost by the USS Roper on April 15, the first German loss during the coastal campaign. A full convoy system, which included a blackout, was introduced in May. Ten Royal Navy Corvettes and 24-armed trawlers from the Royal Navy were transferred to America's east coast. The Royal Canadian Navy also set up patrols off Boston. A

RAF antisubmarine squadron moved to Rhode Island, protecting New York Harbor. Canadians as well as the British took over Caribbean patrolling. [19] The loss along the coast was dramatic.

The total shipping losses in the rest of 1942 was the greatest of all the wars - 700,000.235 tons in June, 729.160 in October. Shark's unreadable text meant that the U-Boats could operate freely as they please. Even though losses have fallen, increased security off the coast has not made them as dangerous as their counterparts further out at sea. There was no other way.

Bletchley had attracted the USA's attention long before Pearl Harbor. In January 1941, two US Army officers and two other Navy officers visited the station for ten day. They had brought a copy of the Japanese "Purple", a cypher-machine, and taken with them a stack documents and a paper Enigma sim (as well a naval radio direction finding unit similar to the ones used by the British). Admiral King might be reluctant to hear about Station X. But the US military's cryptological offices were certain to. The facility was not like anything they had. In exchange for building faster bombes, they were allowed full access in July

1942. Turing provided the blueprints for his bombe design to US Navy. $2 million was approved by September to support research on a new design. Bletchley, US Navy codebreaking center, OP-20G, signed an US-UK agreement on October 2. They then had to wait several months for the improved bombe to design and go into production. Leaders on both the Atlantic and Pacific sides wondered how many ships would be left.

But, then, in October, another pinch. U-559 was spotted off the Egyptian coast by an RAF Sunderland Patrol plane just after dawn, October 30. Sunderland called five destroyers. HMS Hero the first, which forced the submarine to dive mid-morning, was the first. For the next 16 hour, the ships beat the boat with water-charges. After dark, damage finally brought her back to life. Unfortunately for her, she came up close to HMS Petard. HMS Petard immediately opened firing with her light AA gun. The U-Boats were already panicking and started to abandon ship. Three members of Petard's crew - one of whom was a NAAFI[4] food service assistant - immediately jumped into he sea and swam directly to the submarine. Lieutenant Anthony Fasson & Able

Seaman Colin Grazier climbed down to the hull and found the key settings of October and November. They also found the Short Weather Code Book. These were handed to Tommy Brown (NAAFI assistant) and they then returned to the M4 themselves. The machine was still in their hands and they were still trying get it out. However, the U-Boat with the damaged engine suddenly crashed into the water. Brown, who had been in the conning tower with the documents, was found in the river. Amazingly, they remained dry. They could have been ruined by one drop of water. They were printed on pink paper with red water-soluble Ink. They were kept safe by Turing until a boat brought them back.

The Short Weather Code was very similar to the Short Signal. It allowed U.Boats transmit regular weather reports in an easy-to-understand format. Short signals were not sent unless there was something that was important. Each boat sent multiple weather reports to Shark several times daily. The reported weather was then retransmitted by St. Nazaire. Sometimes, it was even in clear. Bletchley then had the Short Weather Code to use and could build safe cribs suitable for Shark traffic. They had an easy way to get in to U-Boat messages, even without a fast 4-rotor bombe. December's shipping lost were less than half those of November and, after a blip March and April 1943, they never reached 300,000. tons a month. Late 1943, any month that exceeded 100,000 tons was considered to be a bad one.

Bletchley, in December 1942 was asked to send an American liaison officer. Turing was chosen because he knew so much about the bombe that he had written it. He was then taken by the National Cash Register Corporation to Dayton. Ohio and were shown the prototype US Navy nuclear bomb. The prototype US Navy bomb was shown to the public with 64 drums simulating 16 M4 machines. There was also a built in printer that printed details of each stop. It was also 35 times faster to turn the drums at 1,750rpm than the first British bombe. OP-20 G said that they were planning to build 336 drums to reach the fastest breaks. One for each rotor ordered. Turing explained the use of Banburismus to reduce that order and it was reduced to just 96. [20] In final, 121 US Navy aircraft were built. Many were also shipped to Britain. Most British bombes have been moved out from Bletchley, to remote sites that are linked via secure telegraph cables. This is done to lessen the possibility of air raid damage. The Park could now use bombs made in the USA through a transatlantic encrypted cable. The US started testing the bombes on May 3, 1943. By June, there were two running and they had already broken their first Kriegsmarine Keys. From then to the end, a steady flow of intercepts, cribs, recovered keys and deciphered communications flowed back-and-forth between Bletchley & OP-20 -G.

Turing, who was still in the USA when he left, went on to Bell Labs. A team was currently working on a different idea he had, a voice scrambler which could be used on telephone lines. This seems to have excited his interest. He didn't go back to Hut 8 to continue his work, but he acted as floating cryptanalyst while he was away. He was averse to routine, and Shark's conclusion made it seem boring. It was time for a fresh challenge. He found it at Radio Security Service. This agency, also known as Her Majesty's Government Communications Centre is charged with providing secure communications for British government. Turing had made a complete circle. After breaking enemy codes, he was now creating friendly systems. He continued working on scramblers systems throughout the war, both at RSS (and in the USA at Bell Labs). SIGSALY, which he had designed on his first visit to Bell in 422, was bought by the US Army. This was a huge scrambler unit (it weighed in excess 50 tons) and was used to transmit the most important communications information. A dozen were built in all. The first was installed in The Pentagon with an Extension to The White House. The next went into Selfridge's basement in London where General Eisenhower maintained his headquarters. Winston Churchill also used this basement.

Turing also created a more compact device, called Delilah. It could be transported in a large briefcase because it was light and small. Delilah was developed during wartime, and was never adopted. But it was an excellent learning experience. Donald Bayley who is an electronics expert was also a major contributor to this project. He taught Turing lots about electronics. This was to become very important later.

Ironically Turing resigned from Bletchley Park, as another project that he had initiated began to produce results. A lot of the German high-level traffic was not encyphered on Enigma. Instead it used secure Teleprinter links and the highly complex Lorenz SZ machine. Tunny was the key. Turing devised a method to work out the rotor settings. Turing's priority in that time was Shark. Banburismus was also used against Lorenz. Tommy Flowers was an electrical engineer at Post Office Research Station. He introduced the Tunny crew to him in order to help them. He had already introduced Flowers and Max Newman to Flowers. Then, after Newman's return to Hut 8 and the terror of U-Boats cyphers, the Tunny Team began developing their own version. Heath Robinson[5] was the first attempt. It was a bizarre skeletal contraption using punched tape, light sensors, and key settings to work out key settings. Although it worked, it was slow-reliable. There could be potential in it for flowers. The most problems with the device were in its electromechanical parts. The device's limited electronics functioned much better. He developed an improved version in his spare time that removed many of these moving parts and added more electronics. Heath Robinson's device had approximately a dozen valves. Flowers's new device used 1,600 of these and ran much faster. Colossus, a name given to the prototype because of its complexity and size, was successfully tested at PO Research Station on Dec 8, 1943. After that, it was dismantled by the PO Research Station and taken to Bletchley Park. It and the nine additional 2,400-valve models following were used to break Tunny traffic for the rest of World War II. But, they were capable of much more. Because it was entirely electronic, any instructions could be loaded into it via its tape reader. This made it the first fully programmeable electronic computer. It was a Turing Machine.

Chapter 11: Peacetime

Millions of veterans and war workers started to return home and demobilize when the Second World War ended. Many of them were full of stories about their experiences, and they would share these stories for decades over a pint of beer at their local Royal British Legion Club. The armed services began to decline back towards their peacetime strength as the hostilities -only soldiers, sailors, or airmen began rebuilding their interrupted life.

GC&CS also started shedding staff. On May 8, 1945, Enigma had stopped working. The Japanese Section was finished on September 2. Wrens who were responsible for the bombes were assigned to other units. Civilian workers were often paid off, and security teams meticulously cleaned out the Park's extensive archives. The majority of documents and machines were destroyed. In 1946, GC&CS changed its name to Government Communications Headquarters. It moved to Eastcote. It moved again to Cheltenham in 1951. There it remains today, in a huge, donut-shaped building. The Park was abandoned and sold. Its staff was also dispersed.

None of them spoke.

The Official Secrets Act was a binding law that bound them and encouraged loyalty to their team. They remained silent until 1974, although some survivors refuse to talk. There were good causes for that. Soon after the guns stopped in Europe the tension between the western Allies' and Stalin's USSR started to rise. Churchill and Attlee were aware that breaking Soviet codes could prove vital. They didn't want Stalin to find out their capabilities, as he was notoriously paranoid.

There was also the rest. It became obvious by the mid-1940s that most of Britain's extensive colonies would soon become independent. But, the mother state wanted to keep an ear on them. There was an easy way out. British had already captured U-110 M3, their first Enigma computer, in May 1941. The British had over a dozen Enigma machines at the end. The surrender followed. The British occupation zone captured almost a quarter Germany. In it, there were hundreds upon hundreds of air stations, army headquarters, and major railway stations. (which also had Enigmas). British ownership held a significant portion of the

German fleet (including dozens U-Boats). They had suddenly thousands upon thousands Enigma machines. Many were damaged and many were older, or less common models. Nevertheless, they contained hundreds of Enigma I models and M3s. These were later refurbished and passed over to newly independent countries of the British Commonwealth. They were unbreakable and the best cyphermachines in the world, the British assured. Only a few of the surviving bombes spun at Cheltenham.

Bletchley Park remained secretive, which allowed for valuable intelligence tools to be preserved. But it made it difficult and costly to award Park's successes. Winston Churchill said Turing made a single most significant contribution to the Allied win [21] and it was worthy recognition. However, it had to remain discreet. In 1945, the King gave Turing the Order of the British Empire. He was also offered a job as a scientist at the National Physics Laboratory. This opportunity would have allowed him to build upon the work that Tommy Flowers had done with Colossus.

In 1943, the USA built an enormous electronic computer known as ENIAC. It was nearing completion in 1945, and the British wanted to keep up with it. The NPL was tasked with creating and building its own computer. Turing's post-War work on computed numbers qualified him for the position. His previous work at Bletchley and Bell Labs as well as RSS was what secured the deal. In January 1946, he presented to the NPL Executive Committee his design for a stored programme computer. But his colleagues didn't – couldn't – know about Colossus so they were skeptical that Turing's design would succeed. He knew it would. But he couldn't tell them how. Tommy Flowers, who was also interested in the actual engineering, was again blocked by security. He did not convince him and instead built the Pilot Model ACE first as a test machine.

ENIAC (the US computer) was created in February 1946. It started operating less than a year after Turing's presentation. EDVAC (a more powerful successor) was already being constructed. That placed pressure on NPL. They knew that such computers were essential for designing hydrogen bombs. USA had backpedaled on their cooperation agreement to establish the Manhattan Project. Now, they wanted to ban Britain from any further development of nuclear weapons. This was unacceptable by the UK so a functioning computer was necessary.

Turing was right when he predicted that the Pilot ACE would power up on May 10, 1950. EDVAC used subroutines. These were pre-programmed tasks that could be used in a variety of ways. It was faster to create programs. It also used a structured programming language known as Abbreviated Computing Instructions. This provided a standardized way to write code. EDVAC required customized code for each task. Pilot ACE ran at a speed 1Mhz and could store 384 instructions. Each instruction consisted of 32 bits. It was the fastest machine in the world.

It didn't maintain that status for too long. EDVAC became operational in 1951. It was more difficult to program than the Pilot ACE. It also had more memory and a higher speed. It was upgraded substantially by 1958. NPL had already built MOSAIC by that point, which was an improved version ACE. It was activated between 1952 and 1953. The story of its career is still kept secret, but it is probable that it did ultimately help design Britain's first hydrogen weapon. The ACE design ultimately became the basis to the Bendix G-15 personal computing system.

Turing was no longer with the NPL at the time Pilot ACE was established. He returned to Cambridge late in 1947 frustrated at the restrictions on his access to information. He then wrote his first speculative paper regarding artificial intelligence. While the paper was not published until much later, it laid the groundwork for much of his work.

In 1949, he accepted an offer to be a senior researcher at University of Manchester. In 1949, he became the deputy director for the university's computer laboratory. They were developing a better computer. Turing was able to create software for the computer, even though the design was already beyond its theoretical stage. The Manchester Mark 1 ran on June 16, 1949. Its patents featured 34 new features. Many were later adopted by IBM mainframes. British academics also became disenchanted by it. When the machine was first reported, the press called it an electronic brain. This led many to question whether a machine could ever be truly intelligent. Turing was convinced it was possible. He began work on the most important paper of his career. It was published October 1950 in Mind, a prominent journal of philosophy and psychology.

Computing Machinery and Intelligence began in a blunt statement. "I propose to examine the question, Can machines think 22] He calmly and clearly defined "think," "machine," and explained the ways a digital computer could perform all the functions of a mind. Finally, he mercilessly demolished any objections to his argument. He then suggested an artificial intelligence standard test.

The Turing Test has a simple yet powerful design. Turing suggested that a machine would be intelligent if it could trick a human into believing they were interfacing, which Turing did. He suggested that the interrogator, who is human, be placed in a single room. This would allow them to communicate with the computer by using an output device. (Monitors were not common in the 1960s - most computers used punched tape or dials for their output). To keep the experiment impartial, the interrogator shouldn't be asked whether they were talking directly to a machine. Instead they should be asked if it was a man or woman. The experiment would continue several times. The interrogator might interact with the machine and occasionally with a real human to hide their true gender. If they incorrectly guess when they are talking to the machine as they do when talking with a human, then the machine is intelligent.

The Turing Test is now accepted as the main hurdle a computer must overcome to be considered intelligent. Despite many public claims (most recently, on June 7, 2014), the Turing Test has not been successfully passed. [23] All claims of success have been based on a program that analyzes syntax and vocabulary to determine the best answer from a collection. The program doesn't actually have intelligence. Instead, it uses pattern recognition. They have used other tricks to cover up awkward replies. In 2014, an interrogator was told that they were talking about a Ukrainian teenager. So any strange answers would have to be interpreted as English unfamiliarity. You would get a different result by asking it in Ukrainian. To pass the test legally, the machine must be able comprehend the concept. It is not yet possible, but it is on the horizon.

Chapter 12: Downfall

Turing's interest in biology grew in the latter half of 1951. Genetics was still very young, but mathematics was already able to be used to make it easier. Turing was intrigued by how living things shape themselves as they evolve from a single cell into a complex organism. His theory of pattern formation in development organisms was developed without the need to experiment in a lab and rely solely on equations. It was tested experimentally by University of Pennsylvania scientists. [24]

Turing published Turing's hypothesis in 1896. James Watson and Rosalind Fenner, Rosalind Franklin, explained the structure for the DNA molecule. It is the chemical that controls development and heredity. DNA is often called a code or a languages. It isn't. It's just one molecule that can catalyze numerous complex chemical reactions. The end product is proteins. Because it behaves very similar to code in some ways, "Code" can be used as a shorthand. Turing could have contributed a lot to the understanding of it and to developing the new science, genetics. He was quickly out of time.

Turing had lived in and worked in sheltered areas his entire adulthood, ever since he came out to his parents. Bletchley was actually where he briefly had a relationship with Joan Clarke a Hut 8 cryptoanalyst. He proposed to her in 1941. After telling her a few weeks later that he was having "homosexual tendencies", she was not dismayed and they continued to be together. He took her on vacations and days off, and bought her a diamond ring. She kept it secret from work. He even suggested that they have children. [25] Turing feared that his sexuality would endanger the marriage and ended the engagement.

Now, he was working out in the real world. Manchester University was very distinct from the isolated atmosphere of Cambridge, or Bletchley Park's eccentric environment. Turing didn't live with the Hut 8 and King's College. Instead, he was living alone in suburban suburbs, dining at home and in local restaurants. He knew he was subject to the law and was now aware of it. He hadn't had much to worry about criminality, except the risk of some unfortunate thieves who might want to take his temperamental bike. Manchester was another story.

Turing was walking along central Manchester's streets in December 1951 just after he had begun his work on biology. Turing encountered a young man near the Oxford Road cinema. Turing was impressed by their conversation and invited them to have lunch. Later, he asked Arnold Murray, the young man, to come over to his house. Murray didn't appear, but in January 1952, they met again and quickly began a relationship.

Turing made the wrong choice, perhaps because of his safe lifestyle. Murray took PS10 (roughly $11,150 in 2014 dollars) from Turing's wallet. When Turing confronted Murray about it, Murray was able half-convinced that he wasn't responsible. Murray was still suspect of being involved when the house was broken into on January 23. [26]

Turing then moved onto thin-ice. He reported the burglary the police. While this was reasonable, and clear up rates were far greater than today, it brought law enforcement dangerously close and his private life couldn't take much scrutiny. The police went to his house, took fingerprints, and started looking through his records. Turing sent Murray a letter, informing him that the relationship was over. He also brought up the question of the missing money. Murray, furious, turned up at Murray's doorstep, and denied any knowledge of the cash. They finally came to an understanding. Murray confessed that he was suspicious of Harry, a friend of his who is unemployed, for breaking into the house. Turing's fatal mistake was then.

Murray was still suspected of the burglary. Murray wrapped up the glass he had been using and handed it to him along with a story telling how he obtained it. The risk was not worth it. Police had already determined that Harry was the burglar by the fingerprints they found in the house. Turing's account raised new suspicions. They began questioning Turing. The interrogation started out mildly, and then became more pointed. Turing was shy and awkward and couldn't handle the situation. He eventually admitted to homosexuality in an attempt stop the questions. He was instantly arrested for "Gross Indecency".

A section 11 of the United Kingdom Criminal Law Amendment Act of 2018 provided a vague paragraph, which allowed for upto two years' imprisonment for men found guilty of gross indecency. This could apply to any man found guilty of indecency with another person in public or privately. The law didn't explain what the offence really was, but everyone understood that it meant gay indecency. [6] Section 11 had been used in 1895 to send Oscar Wilde into Reading Gaol. It was now used against Alan Turing.

Turing's trial was held on March 31, and Turing's defense should have been strong. He was called "national asset" because of his work on computing. His OBE was also mentioned, along with details about crucial war work that couldn't been revealed. Guy Burgess & Donald Maclean had been identified as Soviet spies. But, it was clear that there was little tolerance for a man perceived as just another Cambridge-educated "poofter" who had a lot of secrets and should not have been trusted. In strict legal terms, he had already admitted to the "offence" to detectives looking into the burglary. In an effort to lower his sentence, the defendant pleaded guilty.

This strategy may have worked. He could have been sentenced two years imprisonment with no alternatives. Instead, he was allowed to choose:

he could opt for probation and hormone treatment. He accepted.

The hormone treatment was to inject synthetic estrogen in order to decrease the libido. It is meant to reduce sexual urge during the treatment, but one is supposed return to normal when it is completed. Two weeks after the trial, he wrote to a close friend: "I hope they're correct." [27] But his daily life could never go back to normal.

British law made homosexuality a crime. But in Turing's world, it was taken more seriously. It was possible to blackmail homosexuals and, if they held valuable secrets, it made them easy targets of foreign spies. It seems that no one ever thought that gay men could be blackmailed. If they were exposed, they could face criminal charges. Instead, their response was to be removed from any position handling sensitive data. Although members of the Armed Forces could be administratively removed as late in 2000, 32-years after homosexuality was declared illegal, there was no chance of them passing security vetting. Turing, who had been in the top ranks of security clearances ever since 1938, was now expelled. After six years at the heart the intelligence services, and then working for the nation's top technology projects, the door was closed on Turing forever.

Turing continued to research biology for two years but his heart stopped. He also suffered horrible side-effects due to the "therapy," that turned out to be chemical Castration. He began to feel depressed and his breasts grew from the estrogen injections. It got so bad that he had to go to therapy. This was a significant and difficult step in early 1950s. It appears that he had had enough.

Turing's cleaner became concerned by the silence in the home and opened the door to his bedroom on June 7, 1954. She found him unconscious in his bed. An autopsy revealed that cyanide poisoning was responsible for the death. But cryptographic genius had left one final puzzle unsolved. How was this possible?

Turing had been doing experiments that involved electroplating teaspoons filled with gold. He was using a solution consisting of gold dissolved into potassium cyanide. This legal purchase was made legally from a chemical provider. Turing also had a home-built apparatus in his spare area. There is speculation that the device was releasing hydrogen cyanide gas. Turing stumbled through his bedroom before collapsing. [28] On the bedside desk, was a small, almost symbolic apple. Most people believe that it was cyanide-injected. It is most likely for two reasons. Hydrogencyanide is a powerful blood agent and Turing could not have escaped if he accidentally poisoned him with it. Turing's favourite fairy tale was Snow White. The 1937 Disney version of the story featured a scene where the Wicked Queen drinks poison from an apple. [29]

Alan Mathison Turing passed away on June 12, 1955. He didn't use the Enigma machine to keep his final secrets.

Chapter 13: Rehabilitation

In the sixty years since Alan Turing's demise, society has experienced a profound transformation. It is unlikely that the relationship that ended his professional career and ultimately his personal life would be discussed in Britain today. His security clearance would have not been affected. Turing was treated terribly for all the good he had done for his country. And it took a long while before the government officially recognized that. But, eventually it did happen. An online petition for a late apology garnered over 30,000 signatures in 2009, many of them from well-known scientists. It was heard. Prime Minister Gordon Brown of Canada, described Turing's treatment as "horrifying", and "utterly inequitable" on September 10, that year. He then apologized on behalf all citizens. Turing deserves so much better. His reputation, which had been lost for so many decades, was starting to come back after TIME Magazine placed him among the 100 most important persons of the 20thcentury. The momentum to officially remove his name was increasing. A petition asking for a formal pardon was filed in 2011. It received 37,000 names. However, it was not accepted by his supporters. In 2011, a group of peer, including ex-Hut 8 language expert Lady Trumpington introduced a bill at the House of Lords asking for action. Before the bill could be passed through Parliament, Queen Elizabeth II made a royal pardon.

Turing was controversially pardoned. There is no doubt that he was guilty, under the law in his day. This law is still unjust. In striking proof of his immense influence, however, most of this controversy took place online. Tim Berners Lee was the first to create the World Wide Web. DARPA laid the foundation, but modern computers are rooted back to Turing's 1936 and 1946 papers. His efforts are the basis of the connected society we live in today.

We have the freedom that we enjoy. The freedom we enjoy isn't infinite and there are some restrictions that make it difficult. But the world is freer now than it was if Admiral Donitz's U–Boats had beaten Britain to submission and made Hitler Europe's ruler. Although it's unlikely that either Japan or Germany would have taken the USA, would the USA have been able to survive in open democracy if it faced militarized fascist imperialist empires on both the east or west?

Alan Turing was the one who made it possible.

Anomaly

"Among awkward, geeky teenagers, Alan Turing is a patron angel. He was never a part of the mainstream, but achieved these remarkable feats as part in a secret queer history of computer science - Graham Moore screenwriter of 2014's The Imitation Game

Julius Mathison Turing (39) and Ethel Sara Stoney (31) were most likely the ones who conceived Alan Mathison Turing. Ethel was very pregnant at the time, so she decided to fly back to India for her second baby. Ethel entered a Warrington Crescent nursing house in West London on June 23rd 1912 and was soon to become the father of computer science and codebreakers. John Ferrier, John's elder brother, was, however, born in Coonoor (British India's Tamil Nadu) in 1908. Alan was baptized in July 2007.

It is said that hardship breeds greatness. Although they weren't wealthy, the Turings were more than happy and were unaffected in the wake of the global economic crash that decimated millions.

An image of 3-year-old Alan is widely circulated. He is pictured wearing a miniature sailor costume and the same deep sides he would use throughout his life. It shows an adorable, well-adjusted child who seems happy and cheerful. Another picture of Alan, his brother John and their barefoot relationship by the beachline adds to the misleading facade. The boys were content to sleep in comfortable beds and eat a full meal each night. But their home life was anything else. Julius was a Madras Presidency officer (also known "Presidency of Fort St. George") of the Indian Civil Service. He returned home to India in September 1912. Ethel followed her lead, leaving her young men in the care and supervision of several friends. The majority of their time was spent in a beautiful, unpretentious brick manor located on Baston Lodge at East Sussex. They shared it with Colonel Ward and Mrs. Ward.

Alan's eccentricities, from the very beginning, were well-recognized by those around him. His foster mom, for example, frequently groaned about the boy's quirks. Ethel later saw the child's brutal honesty and recalled it to her. She left her luggage at the front entrance to say goodbye to her boys. However, she reminded Alan (aged 3) to behave in her absence. The child responded, "I will." "But sometimes I'll forget!"

Alan sought solace from Nanny Thompson, a grandmotherly warm woman in this strict family. She loved the boy despite the fact that he had other interests and was not a typical person. But she didn't forget about the child's quirky traits. Thompson later stated to Turing's biographer Andrew Hodges "You couldn't camouflage him anything." "I do remember Alan and my playing together. He saw it, and I played so he would win. There was some commotion for several minutes.

The story reveals that the child's intelligence was far beyond his years. He actually taught himself how to read by using Reading Without Tears (19th-century illustrated children's book), published by FavellLee Mortimer. It took him just three weeks. He began to become obsessed with math, numbers and puzzles. Alan requested an Atlas for his 4th Birthday. After receiving his present, the child went into his room and admired the complex maps and pictures for hours.

Edwin Tenney Brewster's Natural Wonders Everyone Child Should Read sparked the curious child's interest in all things science. This 51-page picture book was encyclopedic. It covered scientific and natural phenomena such as "How the Chicken Gets in the Egg", "How we Differ from the Animals" and "Where do We Do Our Thinking," among other topics. Once he learned how to write, his observations and observations about any topic that interested him began to be recorded in his journals. He was also fascinated at the exactitude required in formulas or recipes, and dedicated several journals to it. He also included a nettlesting cure that required crushed Dock leaves in his collection.

Perhaps the Wards did not approve of Alan's endless questions, but he grew up to seek out his own answers. Young Alan was a reflective boy. He liked educational books more than adventure novels. He also enjoyed reading multiple texts about the same topic. Alan was most obsessed with numbers. Ethel described Alan as "always] interested with figures - not in any mathematical association – before he could read, would study the serial number on lamp posts etc."

It's easy to assume that the boy was more attentive then his high-spirited and distracted peers. Once, the clever child ran away from a family picnic. He walked behind a group flying bees. After returning about an hour later, he had a small jar with fresh honey. He shared it with his brother. Although this is true, Alan, a young boy, struggled to understand simple concepts such a calendar. He later admitted that his brain was not able "to predict when Christmas would fall ...[and that it did so at regular intervals."

Alan was 6 years old when he first enrolled at St. Michael's Day School in Hastings. Here he remained until age nine. There are conflicting stories about his performance in this school. Some said that he did not do well, while others stated that he impressed and impressed his headmistress. He reportedly once wrote: "I have known clever boys and hardworking men, but Alan's genius is the best."

Alan moved to Hazelhurst Preparatory School when he turned 9. This was a small school with 36 boys ranging in age from 9 to 13. His newfound passion for chess, and his passion to learn more about numbers, helped him blossom further at Hazelhurst Preparatory school. He enjoyed spending his time playing chess with his brother and Ward kids, as well as poring over his notebooks and textbooks. Ethel shared the story of Alan, who "always sought to understand the underlying principles...having learned how find the square root from a given amount at school, he later deduced for his own how to determine the cube roots."

Hazelhurst, however, was not an institution that valued science or mathematics. Instead, Hazelhurst taught Greek, Latin and other subjects to prepare students for the exclusive private school Alan and his parents planned for. They were less concerned about Alan's science and mathematics passion than they were about his careless spelling or lackadaisical attempts in grammar.

Alan's father was honored to have served with the Indian Civil Service from 1924 to 1924. However in order to ease the taxation on his annuities, the son decided to relocate to France where Ethel joined him. Fortunately, Alan, 12 years old, was less upset by the news because he had grown accustomed to their absence. The boy could become lonely, but he was able look after himself. For instance, he would get lost and need a ride from school so he rented a taxicab. He even tipped the drivers.

Alan, aged 14, joined his brother in Sherborne School. The all-boys private boarding college was located in Dorset. The charming teenager was very handsome but was not worried about his looks. However, the academy was keen to see boys who were like him and clean up their lives. Sharp flannel shirts and crisp ties were the perfect replacement for his wrinkled, short-sleeved, and grey-colored sweaters. This was his first day in Sherborne. He had his shirt tied neatly and his ensemble ironed. Unfortunately, fate didn't want to make him look so elegant. Alan woke up to discover that all railway services had been cancelled due to the general strike. He didn't let the lackluster cabs or the crowds of picketers deter him. Instead, he ordered a telegram for his new headmaster to be sent. The message informed him of the current situation and assured him of his arrival on the next day. He then rode his bicycle 63 miles to Sherborne from Southampton, stopping at Blandform Forum Crown Hotel for a quick break. The staff were so touched by the persistence of the teenager that several of their employees wished him goodbye at the cracking of dawn the following morning. His inspiring story was even published in the local paper.

Alan was enthusiastic about his education. However, he was less than ideal for the dull environment at Sherborne. Sherborne, just like the preparatory schools, placed emphasis on classical subjects. Scientific subjects were only given two hours each week. Alan was an obscure boy, with a chronic fetish of science and a reputation for wallowing in darkness. Geoffrey O'Hanlon - the housemaster of Westcott House, where Alan stayed - commented that Alan was a shy boy with a passion for science and spent much of his time investigating advanced mathematics. "If he intends to stay at [private] high school, he must make an effort to learn. If he wants to become a specialist in science, he's wasting his time at [private]school." O'Hanlon, according to reports, told Alan many times that only the "stupidest" of minds can imagine that scientific discovery leads us to the answers to the riddles of this universe.

His teachers didn't have much of a positive opinion about him. John, Alan's brother, claims that Alan was continually nag by his mother through letters and her visits in return for the often scathing remarks made on Alan's reports cards. A. H. Trelawney Ross made one such comment about Alan. It read, "I can forgive his writing, though I find it the worst I have ever encountered" and "I try to tolerate his...slipshod work...but I cannot forget the stupidity of him attitude towards sane discourse on the New Testament." He was at bottom of his English class in that year. As expected, Alan did not fare well in Latin. He was second-to-last in his batch. The comments made by Ross, his Latin teacher were equally sharp: "He oughtn't to be taking this course as far is form subjects." Ross found it a distasteful thing that Alan used to do algebraic and other mathematics behind the walls of literature and open religion, which only made Ross more disgusted.

One could assume that Alan was admired by his science and mathematics teachers, but he often felt unmotivated. But this doesn't mean that he wasn't a gifted, even unorthodox mathematician. Alan was said to have amazed his teachers by solving complicated calculus equations without ever having received any training. While his instructors supported the original solutions Alan created to traditional problems as an option, they took issue with his "dirty working" and inability for class to concentrate. He was too busy figuring out his complicated riddles and equations that he couldn't focus on classes. The same thing happened with his chemistry teacher. He ignored his instructions and did his experiments.

Alan's Sherborne academic achievements were marked by his sporadic displays remarkable competency. Alan did his best work and got excellent grades whenever he felt like doing so. Naturally, his teachers were puzzled by how much more Alan could achieve if they applied themselves. His brother shared the following: "On one notable occasion, was 22nd out the 23 on the term's works, first in the exams and third in the combined results."

Alan must have felt a rush in spite of his poor Sherborne performance. Victor Beuttell (an old friend at the school) was an eminent scientist who shared a common interest in astronomy. Alan was invited to find the right curvature for even illumination. The story goes that Alan did more. Alfred didn't know about the importance of the thickness in the glass for illumination.

Alan's relationship at this stage with his parents was difficult, but not unusual given his age. John would later say that Julius was not aware of Alan's "strange behaviors" or his poor school records, but that he simply ignored them. Ethel, however, was always on Alan's case, "forever exasperated" with his refusal to keep his kempt clean, his crude manners, as well as other insignificant foibles. Ethel claimed in her biographie that she detected Alan's intelligence above average early on. John disagreed. John stated that Ethel was not doing anything to encourage him to follow a conventional path. It's obvious that her efforts to make Alan as unique as possible were futile.

The teenager was unaffected by his dissidents and continued on his own, divergent path. Alan's compulsive experiments and madcap capers were the ones that really upset his family. Alan was like many his age, not only did he love mathematics and science, but he also had occasional whims. John recalls his unsuccessful attempt at conquering the violin. He said that it was an "excruciating" period. However, he never gave up on something he wanted.

Alan gave up swimming, canoeing and all other summertime activities while the brothers were in Dinard northwestern France. He brought his haul of seaweed to the cellar, burned it, and then extracted a few precious drops from the ashes through boiling water. Finally, he put the murky brown droplets into a vial before presenting it to Sherborne's science guru.

Alan began to experiment with breeding red banana flies using separate test tubes. This was months later. Alan set out to reproduce Gregor Mendel's encounters with the pests so that he could better understand the workings genetics. He failed to properly seal his tubes in time for his investigations. However, the insects took advantage of this and began harassing the family for many days. Housemaster O'Hanlon recalled another time when Alan skipped several of his classes. The teacher who later found him found him "boiling heaven's secrets witches' blend by the aids of two guttering candlesticks on a naked wood sill."

Alan's fascination for these subjects grew, and his ability to master them was amazing for someone any age. The 16-yearold received a new copy of Albert Einstein's The Theory of Relativity in 1925 from his grandfather as a gift for Christmas. Alan read through the book in less that a week. He then made a note of all the details and kept it in a notebook. Ethel did not understand what he was doing. He showed the notebook to his mother, hoping to get her to see this topic he had so deeply loved. Ethel was soon informed by Alan's mathematics instructor that "there wasn't much more he could do for [Alan]" and that "he would need to go on his own." The Turing Digital Archive has it.

Ethel continued nagging Alan into adulthood as do many mothers, but his guardians and family eventually let him go. They observed the teenager's withdrawing and strange behavior. His habit of wearing full-costume private soldier costumes and marching down to Knightsbridge barracks in scorching summer heat was a clear sign. However they lost interest in his other bizarre activities. John explained, "[He] was...good for beating the system, but of course, he did more odd things than anyone else, so it was less likely that one would inquire into them."

Not surprisingly, Alan was less understanding of his schoolmates. Biographical films have exaggerated Alan's quirks to make dramatic effect. They include his asocial behavior and famous stutter. In reality, his speech difficulties were mild and his stammer was mostly caused by his unique speech patterns. He spoke very slowly and chose his words carefully, which was a characteristic that frustrated journalists seeking to interview him. Alan loved his own company, but he was actually close to his friends.

The pain and suffering inflicted on him by bullies at school was, regrettably, not a pleasant one. While the majority of the bullying occurred at Hastings High School, the hurt he felt was irrevocable. To make matters worse, his tormentors frequently stuffed him into the crawlspaces empty classrooms, then secured all loose floorboards shut.

Many experts today believe Alan was Asperger's. Ben MacIntyre, Michael Fitzgerald, and Henry O'Connel all count among these experts. In 2003, the pair concluded that Alan satisfied all six criteria of the Gildberg criteria for the syndrome. They included "severe impaired in reciprocal interpersonal interaction, all-absorbing narrow interested, impositions and interests (onself or others), verbal communication problems, speech & language problems, motor clumsiness, and nonverbal communication problems."

Ethel has a recounted account which many say shows how inept Alan was about certain topics. Ethel once neglected to read The Pilgrim's Progress aloud to Alan. According to Ethel's 4-year-old son, he cried out, "[You've] spoiled all of it!" He then ran back to his room in a hurry. Alan's hands were stained with ink splotches. But he could not sleep at night unless he had a daily apple. An unabashed school report in 1927 accuses the teenager of his odd mannerisms. He attributed it to his refusal to conform. "His ways sometimes tempt him to persecution: although I don't believe he's unhappy. Incontestably, he doesn't look normal.

A Rising Sun and the Setting Moon

"I want to be in a relationship that lasts forever, and I might feel inclined not to accept anything that could have a temporary nature." - Alan Turing

Alan met his 6th-form Sherborne classmate, who saw through all of the discomfiture and was very happy to be there. This boy was very likely Alan's first crush.

Christopher Morcom was Christopher's name. A sharp-witted 16-yearold, with long hair and a infectious smile, he was called Christopher Morcom. Christopher was kind and a good conversationalist. However it was their shared interest in science, astronomy, math that made them feel like they were a team. Christopher did not hesitate to challenge Alan's opinion, which Alan liked the most. The boys connected more than the puzzles and cryptic ciphers they shared in The Imitation Game (2014). The boys also did extracurricular experiments together and discussed "their" pet problems.

Christopher was an admirable student when it came to academic performance. However, he often found class topics boring, just like Alan. The pair traded notes (sometimes in code), which contained mathematical equations. One of their notes, which they passed in 1929 while attending a French lecture, can now be accessed via the Alan Turing Internet Scrapbook. On one side, you will see two games (tic-tac–toe) of "noughts or crosses", while on the other is rough art referring to the "problem of the equation of parallel lines within Euclidean geometry."

Christopher was, in many aspects, the yin opposite of Alan's Yang. Christopher, who was more methodical but more structured than Alan, helped balance him by reminding Alan that he needed to be more cautious with hazardous chemicals and substances. But, it didn't take away from Alans raw enthusiasm. Christopher was also encouraged beyond his comfort zones by Alan's unconventional but brilliant research and analysis methods.

Christopher appeared to be a positive influence on Alan in more ways than one. Even Sherborne police noticed a shift in Alan. Alan found his spirits lifted and he started to complete his assignments. He also took his examinations seriously. Alan later expressed his admiration for Christopher, saying that he "had great power in practical research of finding out the best way to accomplish anything."

Tragically Alan's best friend was tragically taken from him on Valentine's Day 1930. Christopher died from complications from bovine tuberculosis. It was a disease he contracted several years earlier after consuming contaminated dairy milk. Alan didn't feel much comfort from Dr. Edwin Davis's note to him, the head at Sherborne's mathematics division. He was totally devastated. Alan sent Mrs. Morcom an exquisitely-written sympathy letter on the 18th. "I'm certain that I could not find anywhere else a companion as brilliant and yet so charmingly unconceited." It's hard to believe that you could have had a worse loss.

While romanticized scenes and films have often depicted the couple's relationship, many biographers insist that Christopher considered him a friend. Alan himself made this clear in his letter to Mrs. Morcom. He mentioned that Christopher sometimes felt uncomfortable about Christopher "worship[ing]] [the ground he walked on]." Alan wrote to her: "Chris knew so well how I liked Him, but he hated it."

Christopher was as open and sincere about his friendship with Alan, but his warmth towards him never diminished. He even kept a photo of Christopher framed on his study desk. When asked about it, he stated that it had motivated him to achieve his goals. Christopher made some of the comments that he was afraid to make about the coincidence, but he seemed more open to the idea of having [Alan] around in a passive manner.

Some believe that this event was what made Alan an atheist. The heartbroken teenager couldn't understand the thought that an electric, vibrant mind would be gone in a matter of days. Others contend that Alan was not a believer in organized religion. He attended church services to appease the devout mother. There are others who claim that he subscribed Buddhist beliefs.

The majority of skeptics like Alan would never believe in anything that would suggest life after death. However, Alan's journal shows that he did consider everything. The grief-stricken 17-yearold was traumatized by the loss his dear friend and by the thoughts of death and the complexity that human minds can create. In his diary, he wrote about the premonition he thought he had. Alan fell asleep on his pillow several hours before

Christopher exhaled. He fell asleep as he viewed the clock in a campanile. The spinning hands of the clock were pointing at a quarter to 3. He suddenly felt compelled to look towards the window to the right. There he saw the moon slowly disappearing below the horizon. When he saw this, he knew that it meant a "goodbye, Morcom." Alan was immediately awakened by this thought. In the morning, he learned of Christopher's hospitalization.

Alan wrote it off years later as a pure coincidence. This was almost certainly due to his subconscious. Alan wrote: "It isn't difficult to explain those things away." "But I wonder!"

Alan was probably consumed by grief over Christopher's loss and he began to fantasize about Christopher's mind surviving without a physical vessel. Alan once wrote that the "mechanism" of the body holding the soul is lost and the spirit can find a new one. The body provides something the spirit can use and take care of.

Readers of his work will be able to discern that Alan saw the spirit (and the physical vessel) as two distinct but divisible entities. This, many claim, was the embryonic idea for the "universal machine." In fact, it was his early theories about the possibility of encapsulating the human brain in another body that eventually led him to conceptualize "mental processing."

"I feel that Morcom and I will see each other again, and that there will also be some work for us ...'"," Alan wrote to Mrs. Morcom. "It never came to me to make more friends than Morcom. He made every other person seem so ordinary."

Christopher had everything left to live for at his funeral. While both were gifted, Christopher was the one who had been awarded a full Trinity College Cambridge scholarship. Alan was not eligible for a scholarship. His poor grades almost cost him his chance at the School Certificate (now the GCSE). Christopher's tragic death is believed by many to have been the spark that ignited Alan's passion and drove him to continue his friend's legacy.

Alan was determined to be admitted to Trinity College. His application was rejected and he settled for King's College. This, it turned out, was a blessing. For the first time, he could pursue his childhood passions. With that, he began academically to thrive. Alan's college career began in 1931. One of the highlights was the opportunity for him to study with Professor Godfrey Harold Hardy. Hardy was a legendary number theory and mathematical analyst. Hardy was the Sadleirian Fellow (his professorship was in pure mathematics). His 1940 essay, "A Mathematician's Apology", which was widely praised by experts, is known as "one among the best insights into an working mathematician's thoughts written for laymen."

Hardy

King's College's liberal environment and freedom-thinking culture, is what many consider to be the "oasis for acceptance." King's College became Alan's first "real home" and he felt so at ease that he began to read the New Statesman, an influential leftist publication. Also, he was very involved in the 1933 antiwar movement. Despite its name, Alan dismissed Our Fighting Navy's recruitment piece. He also said that it was "blatant militarist propaganda." Although he held "modernist" views, he wasn't opposed to war. But he believed that citizens should be given the right and power to decide the fate of the country's fighting men. He was elected to the Anti-War Council, a student body that was set up to "organize chemical workers and munitions workers" if war was declared.

King's College provided an opportunity for Alan to explore his sexuality. As many college students do during college, he was open to having a few flings. He even began semi-exclusive relationships. James Atkins, a fellow mathematics major-turned-musician, was one such individual, but while he was a smart, talented soul and pleasant company, he had impossible shoes to fill. Nigel Cawthorne who wrote The Enigma Man said that Alan was "in [Alan]'s] mind...[Atkins] couldn't compare with the lost Christopher." Alan also had a romantic connection to Frederick William Clayton. Clayton was a classically trained linguist and Alan himself described him as "the best-trained man [he]'d ever met."

Their romance faded but their friendship never did. Following the Kristallnacht incident in Nazi Germany in Nov 1938, the pair hosted two Jewish brothers who were smuggled into Germany from Vienna by Quakers Relief Action. Frederick and Alan then rode their bikes furiously through the rain, to Harwhich, the refugee camp where the boys were being protected. Bob Augenfeld (one of the boys) was given to Alan. Frederick would sponsor the other child, "Karl", who went only by "Karl". Alan was attracted to Bob because his father, a former aide-decamp in World War I, was a chemist. Alan made sure Bob was allowed to attend Lancashire Rossall. The respected institution is open to refugees and was free of charge. Alan maintained contact via letters with Bob to show genuine interest in his career and development.

Alan smiled proudly as he wore his dark graduation robes with a flat, diamond-capped cap to receive his undergraduate degree. It was first-class honors. The 23-yearold was made a Fellow of King's College the year after his dissertation "On the Gaussian Error Function", a collection of equations demonstrating "the limitation theorems in the theory or probability" (or the central limit theorem). Alan's work was almost identical to Jarl's, but it wasn't until that point that he realized the truth of his discovery. The paper's emphasis in the paper on the "quasinecessary" condition was what got him admitted.

Alan's Sherborne old friends heard of his achievements. The boisterous children apparently burst into song when they learned.

"Tu-ring,

You must have found it attractive.

To be made a champion,

"So early!

Max Newman, an internationally recognized expert on mathematics, presented a series of important lectures to Alan about the Foundations of Mathematics at Cambridge University. It was during one of the earlier lectures that Alan first encountered the Entscheidungsproblem, or the "decision problem." Newman presented to the attendees three questions posed by German mathematician David Hilbert, which are as follows:

"1. Is mathematics finished?

2. Are mathematicians consistent?

3. Is mathematics decidable?"

Kurt Godel was already proving that mathematics is incomplete and inconsistent at this point. The final question is about whether there is a mathematical process or algorithm that, when applied, to any equation will "take a formal grammar and a statement...that will output a truth or false depending on what the statement's truth value is."

Taking up the challenge, Alan went to work on designing a theoretical contraption that would prove that no such algorithm existed, thereby rendering mathematics "undecidable." This theoretical contraption, dubbed the "Universal Computing Machine," and later aptly named the "Turing Machine," is deconstructed in Alan's 1936 paper, "On Computable Numbers and an Application to the Entscheidungsproblem." Plainly put, this "abstract digital computing machine," equipped with boundless memory, could automatically perform set tasks without the need of a manual (human) operator. Cawthrone explained how the subject was handled with this passage: "What Alan produced was remarkable...When Newman...described Hilbert's

„definite method" as a 'mechanical procedure, he started an Idea In [Alan's] heads...The term 'mechanical' in its original meaning had meant manual occupation...work carried out by human beings. However, mechanical became synonymous with vacuum tubes, rotors, and gears by the 1930s. It was a machine. [Alan] took both meanings to heart."

The machine was modeled on the classic teleprinter. Alan designed a tape that was limitless, so it could support and complete even the most complex computations. A "program" of instructions would govern the machine's actions. It was written in symbols and stored within its infinite memory. In effect, this eliminated the need for a human operator since the machine could be controlled by the program independently. Alan explained how the machine can delete or input symbols to the tape. The other symbols are only rough notes intended to 'assist in the memory.' These notes won't be eraseable.

Gabriel F.'s image of a Turing machines at work

Alan acknowledged on the second pages of his paper the link between his theories of Alonzo and

Church. He wrote: "In Alonzo's recent paper, Alonzo introduced an idea for 'effective calculability.' This is equivalent to my computation, but is very differently defined. Church also reaches similar conclusions about the Entscheidungsproblem." Many believe this acknowledgment was written under the instruction of Newman. Newman was able to convince the Secretary for the London Mathematical Society, to publish Alan's paper. Newman later organized Alan's trip, which took him to Princeton University. Church was his PhD supervisor. Church clearly developed a fondness for his protégé. Church was the one who suggested to Alan to rename the "Turing Machine" and the revered professor did not mind sharing the spotlight. Church even called his thesis "Church Turing Thesis," an expression that still holds today.

Alan found the chance to interact with some the top minds in the field during his spare time. Alan and John von Neumann a Hungarian American mathematician began to work closely in the spring of 1937. The pair had several stimulating conversations about computing. They discussed both the possibilities and limitations of infinite memory, as well the possibilities and possibilities of artificial intelligence. Alan, certain that there would soon be a war against Hitler's dictatorship, built "three of the four stages" a primitive prototype of what he called "electromechanical cryptocurrency-analysis machine" a device that is proficient in binary multiplication.

John von Neumann

Alan's dissertation entitled "Systems of Logic Based Upon Ordinals" earned him his doctorate. Von Neumann offered Alan an assistant position at Princeton. To Von Neumann's disappointment, Alan declined. Instead, he sent him back to Cambridge to renew his fellowship.

Solving an Enigma

"Machines have taken me by surprise with very frequent." - Alan Turing

In the fall, 1939, Alan checked-in to the Crown Inn Shenley Brook End, Buckinghamshire. Mrs. Ramshaw became disapproving as Alan began to carry his suitcases up the stairs. Mrs. Ramshaw noticed a very able-bodied young gentleman who didn't seem to want to join the war effort. Little did she know, this young man's efforts could prove so crucial that historians say he cut down World War II by two to five years and saved potentially 14 million people's lives.

Alan was recruited by the Foreign Office's code-breaking unit secret headquarters to work at the GC&CS's Government Code & Cipher School (GC&CS). Alan marched through Bletchley to report for duty on the 4th of September 1939, just days after Britain declared war against Germany.

Alan's mission in Bletchley Park sounded quite simple. His task was decoding encrypted messages being sent between the German military through their Enigma computers. But, the task of decoding these alien messages appeared impossible at the start. The Enigma machine, Nazi Germany's main encryption system, was also the first to use coding technology. Arthur Scherbius the inventor of the Enigma machine was also the one who created it. In engineering and design sophistication however, the German design trumped all others.

Scherbius was first to try to sell Enigma's invention to the German Navy in April 1918. But he was refused by the Navy because it didn't need the invention. While he sold a few units to the German postal system after the war, the inventor ultimately owes his success largely to Winston Churchill.

Patent for the Enigma Machine

Churchill published The World Crisis, 1923. He described how simple German codes made it possible for the British in World War I to easily locate and sink German shipping. German navy personnel consulted the book, made notes of these statements, then contacted Scherbius once more to get their Enigma machine. "The official history of the German Navy even contained a reference to Churchill's declarations and that "the German Fleet Command, whose radio messages had been intercepted, deciphered and used by the English to play so to speak against the British command." (Kahn 1997, 39).

Scherbius made Enigma machines to support the German navy all through the 1920s. He died before Adolf Hitler was born. In 1929, Scherbius, only 50 years of age, died after his horse-drawn wagon crashed into a wall in the factory. The Enigma manufacturing continued, and the German Navy bought more. The Enigma's popularity increased with the rise of Adolf Hitler, and the expansions in all branches the new Reich military.

Through the 1930s improvements to Enigma technology continued. Scherbius' Enigma contained a basic, letter-only keyboard and three internal motors with 26 position apiece wired together. When you press a key, the first rotating unit will turn to the one that represents a letter. The wiring activated second rotor. This changed the letter yet again and triggered third rotor. This sent a signal to a fixed-half-rotor reflector attached to the machine's wall. It generated a brand new letter. The signal was sent through the rotors again in reverse order and the letter was scrambled three more time. The rotors were moved forward one position each time this happened. This meant that, for example "P" would result with a different encryption for every letter the user wrote. A plugboard was located on the front of each machine to allow manual rewiring.

Scherbius made the rotors removable to allow for further scrambling. The German military as well as the inventor of the code believed it was unbreakable. To decrypt a message, a user needed a key that would reveal the exact starting positions for each rotor. With three rotors at the ready, the number and variety of starting positions was in the trillions. The Wehrmacht quickly increased their number of rotors from three to five. The Navy made seven more. Later in the war, the Germans added eight rotors to the mix, increasing the number possible starting positions to an unbelievable amount.

The official website to the CIA explains that Enigma machines were a cipher. Each keystroke replaced a character contained in the message. This was determined by machine's rotor settings. They also establish a connection between the sender of the message and the receiver. For additional security, the German military services usually double-encrypted their messages by first substituting original text with code words, and then enciphering the encoded text." Due to the machines' utilization of various rotors, coupled with their rambling compendium of code words (transmitted in nonsensical letters and numbers) - switched up every 24 hours - the Enigma could conjure up to 158,962,555,217,826,360,000 different settings.

1943 Enigma machine picture

Monthly Keylist 649 for German Air Force Enigma.

Polish were under attack by Nazi Germany in the West and Soviet Russia (which did not invade them in 1920), to the East. The 1930s saw the Polish feel the most urgent need to crack Enigma to uncover the intentions of their threatening neighbor. Marian Rejewski-Henryk Zygalski and Jerzy Rodzycki, three Polish mathematicians, created the first method to crack Scherbius' Enigma's three-rotor Enigma. "Poles had a brilliant solution. They made a machine from Enigma rotors, wired together so that they could move quickly through the positions and find key patterns. They called it a Bombe. Many commentators believe that the machine's ticking sound was what gave the name to the machine. (Henderson. 2011, 47). As the Germans introduced larger numbers of rotors, Poles lost their ability to build large Bombes that could penetrate complex codes. The Poles invaded Germany and the British took over the codebreaking duties at Bletchley.

At the outbreak of World War I, the British opened their own codebreaking station at

Bletchley Park. Bletchley Park is a large estate in Buckinghamshire. The structure, an architectural mess, was built in the late 19thcentury under the supervision of Sir Herbert Samuel Leon. It served as a location that was relatively safe near key British railway lines.

Draco takes a picture of Bletchley Park

Only a small group of codebreakers were employed by GC&CS - a London-based organization - prior to the war. They cracked the German Enigma older systems. Alfred Dillwyn Knox (the first batch of codebreakers), Peter Twinn (the last of which would later become director of "Hut 6") were among those who were involved. The first "huts," that was a different division within the covert setup, were created only after the war sirens stopped.

Alan was responsible for the management of Hut 8 which was a team that decrypted the messages transmitted by warships and Uboats of Germany. Hugh Alexander was named sector leader after Alan's tenure. Patrick Mahon, a national chess champ, followed him in September 1942.

Turing's place of work before he moved to Hut 8

Hut 8 was always in close collaboration with Hut 4 the division that was responsible for fine-tuning Hut 8's translation and analysis. Alan's tireless crew was essential to his success. The cryptographers were university personnel selected by The Foreign Office. They were also chess savants and winners of the serpentine crossword puzzle contest. Alan worked with Joan Clarke. Harry Golombek. I. J. Good, Peter Hilton, Leslie Lambert, Shaun Wylie amongst others were also heroes. 130 additional women were employed as clerical workers (mainly punching holes on Banbury sheets). Wrens (members Women's Royal Naval Service), were often needed to operate the decryption devices in the hut.

It seemed that the codebreakers were also grateful for the opportunity to work together with Alan. Hilton once boasted that Alan Turing was an "unique" person. What you discover when you get the chance to get to know a genius is the vast difference between a highly intelligent person or a genius. You talk to extremely intelligent people and they give you an idea.

Turing did not give you this feeling. His inventiveness of thought always amazed you. It was remarkable."

Alan was often believed to have been the creator of the Enigma codebreaking machines, but that was not the case. Alan and his crew merely augmented these contraptions. Biuro Szyfrow, also known as "Cipher Bureau," was already present in Warsaw in December 1932. In the seven years to follow, it was the Poles that laid the foundations for the Enigma, which examined and broken down the operational and structural aspects.

Sir Stewart Menzies of MI6 (the UK's Secret Intelligence Service) received word in June 1938 from the Polish Intelligence Service confirming that they had stumbled upon a Polish Jew, who was working secretly at the Berlin Enigma Machines manufacturing plant. The man claimed to have been a skilled engineer and mathematician. He approached the Polish authorities to propose a swap. He would exchange L10,000 for a British passport with French residency and all the information they required about the German machinery, including detailed diagrams and blueprints.

Menzies was suspicious right from the start of the case about the worker in the factory. The chief was convinced that the factory worker was nothing more than a German agent, intent on "[luring]] down the...Britishcryptographic bureau down a blind Alley," and summoned Knox to assist him in vetting the worker. Knox, then, enlisted Alan's aid, who was still working part time at GC&CS. Based on the judgment of the pair, the worker appeared to have a solid background. As such, he was allowed asylum in France. There, he would produce a replica Enigma Machine for them.

Anthony Cave Brown wrote a passage called Bodyguard of Lies about the model. It was connected to two electric typewriters, and to transform a plain-language signal into a cipher text, all the operator had to do was consult the book of keys, select the key for the time of the day, the day of the month, and the month of the quarter, plug in accordingly, and type the signal out on the left-hand typewriter...Electric impulses entered the complex wiring of each of the rotors of the machine, the message was enciphered, and then transmitted to the right-hand typewriter. An operator set up the keys to another similar apparatus according a message and then sent the plain text to the right-hand typewriter.

Before the German cipher, codes were entered manually. However, Knox & Alan discovered that Enigma machines allow for infinite combinations and alphabets of cipher alphabets.

Marian Rejewski from Poland's Cipher Bureau presented what he called the "bomba-kryptologiczna," also known as the "cryptologic bomb" or "cryptologic bomb" in October 1938. This was dedicated towards unraveling Enigma encryption ciphers. The Polish bureau made the vital decision in late July 2012 to reveal to British and French intelligence their existing decryption methods and techniques to the British.

Some say the Poles were stuck in a deadend, and that it took the collective brainpower from their allies to get over the obstacle. This, however, was disputed by Rejewski, who asserted, "No, it was not [technical/cryptologic] difficulties...that prompted us to work with the British and French, but only the deteriorating political situation. We would still, if not more, have shared our achievements as part of the struggle against Germany if there had been no difficulties.

Only after Britain had established contact with the Poles, Alan joined forces with Gordon Welchman to create their bombe. Contrary, the name of the first bombet was not "Christopher," but instead "Victory". It was operational by December 1940. The final product, which was assembled on a large budget of L100,000. (approximately L4million today), was a massive device measuring 6'6", 7 feet, and weighing in at about a ton. It was made up of 36 Enigma Machines, each with its own internal wiring. The machine was activated by all three rotors within the bombe. They moved at a speed equal to Enigma machines. This enabled it to compare sets ciphers with upto 17,500 combinations until a match was found.

Mak Sim's picture at Bletchley, showing a replica of the bombe

Alan and his team had already invented a system they called the Banburismus by the time that the bombe was released. It apparently resulted from an unforeseen error in Enigma's design. Under the Banburismus system, two long strips were cut from paper and dotted with holes by hutcryptographers to represent encrypted messages. To better predict Enigma's rotors' settings, they laid a set of strips on top of each another, also known as "Banbury Sheets." This system was partly responsible for the first breakthrough that occurred on April 26, 1940 when codebreakers successfully decoded maritime messages transmitted by an armoured German trawler, called the Polaris. Other sources credit HMS Arrow in Norway.

Alan's pioneering method revolved around his theory that encrypted messages contained a crib ("a familiar piece of German plain text at familiar points within messages"), and this was what Alan used to prove his point. His methods also depended upon another German error. The weather forecast for the Atlantic was being input in the same format every single day. The codebreakers were also able to identify the origin of the message by listening at their stations. If the location concerned coordinated with weather stations, the word for "wettervorhersage", a German term that means "weather forecast," would appear more often in each message. Similar to what happened with other German signalmen, they often used the same location data and greetings day after day. For example, some sent messages that began with "Heil Nazir" as a greeting. This provided an "crib", which allowed decipherment to the rest.

Another important flaw of Enigma was its inability generate an encrypted letter the same as the letter. A "K" would never be capable of posing as a "K." Chris Smith, a British Telecommunications contributor, pointed out that "The encrypted message could then be lined up with a crib until no other letter lined up as it."

To decipher the Enigma messages in their desks, however, the British codebreakers relied mainly on small errors, scraps information and careful deduction. No matter how technologically advanced or German errors, encryption was still labor-intensive and meticulous. It required both a fanatical work ethic as well as a penetrating mind.

Alan soon discovered that Uboats' weather reports, prior to "encipherment", were encoded on a Wetterkurzschlussel. The Wetterkurzschlussel was short for Wetter Short Signal Book. It compressed their reports into 7 letter messages. Hut 10 broke several "general meteor signals" in February 1941. Alan, his colleagues at Bletchley and his coworkers in Bletchley acquired a 1940 version of the

Wetterkurzschlussel that had been used previously by U-110/MS Munchen. This gave them the ability to clarify the German ships' weather signals and allowed the British to have access to a new set.

As you can see, the British relied on good luck during the war's early years. They also acquired Enigma machines and codebooks in the field, which provided crucial clues about Third Reich transmissions. Although the Germans considered their codes impossible, they changed them periodically. Bletchley was forced to recalibrate their entire operation and even start over. Intelligence coups often arrive in dramatic fashion. The Royal Navy often captured German vessels with Enigmas and codes intact. Captains would usually destroy all cryptographic information before surrendering. However, this was not always the case, as in May 1941. "The German submarine U-110 was brutally attacked by convoys, and severely damaged. She was forced to come to the surface. [...] Fritz Lemp (the boat's commander) ordered the men on board to abandon ship and let her sink. [...] The U-boat's commander, [...] Fritz Lemp, was swimming in the sea and saw the U-boat sinking too slow. He decided to swim back [...] with the intention of destroying the cipher machine. However, the British shot him in the head before he could reach his submarine." (Skwiot. 2006, 48).

The Enigma and code books of U-110, Kriegsmarine-weather ship Munchen and U-33 as well the sub-marine U-33, Krebs the Trawler ("Crab") and many other vessels provided assistance for the exhausted and nearly overwhelmed codebreakers. However, the Germans became increasingly vigilant as they realized that the Allied cryptographers would soon be able to decode their encryption system. In order to shake them off the edge, the Germans added a rotor to their system (now had four), in February 1942. Hut 8's codebreakers had to be left helpless in the dark, suffering a 10 month-long blackout.

Nearly 300,000 tonnes of Allied vessels were being damaged each month due to incapability of the Allied Fleets to anticipate and withstand attacks predicted by Huts 8, and 10. In the first 3 months of 1942, more than 100 vessels were destroyed in the Gulf of Mexico. The British were seeing things get worse.

The heroic actions of three Britons on October 30 1942 were the key to the solution. The British destroyers Petard, Hero Dulverton Pakenham, Hurworth, Hurworth, and Hero ran over the U-559 submarine under Lieutenant Command Hans Heidtmann. They were located near Port Said. U-559 was pursued relentlessly by the British, who dropped numerous depth charges and finally cracked the sub-hull. The German crew abandoned their submarine after being forced to surface near HMS Petard. "Lieutenant Anthony Fasson & Able Seaman Colin Graham swam up to the submarine to recover its signal papers. Tommy Brown [...] was there to help them. Fasson & Grazier were able to escape with the submarine. Both men were given the George

Cross posthumously. Brown was awarded the George Medal." (Copeland (2006), 34).

BletchleyPark published the coordinates on December 13th. They were derived from updated intelligence by the Huts. It took hard work, captured files and machines, as well as Alan's enormous bombes, to enable the Bletchley Park codebreakers keep up to date with the latest developments in Enigma signals from the Germans. It was possible to decode almost every German transmission and allow Churchill's government as well the British Army and Royal Navy remarkable access to the strategic decisions and thoughts of Hitler and his commanders.

Historians believe that these decoded messages played a key role in the Allies' victory in the Atlantic. Now, the cryptographers can be credited with preserving anywhere from 500,000- 750,000 tons Allied shipping.

Naturally, the British intelligence began to share intel details, such as details of espionage and whatever dirt they had regarding the Germans with Office of Strategic Services. This was the United States' answer to the CIA's request. Bletchley Park, codename "ULTRA", provided the most sensitive information - namely decryptions and messages from German ships - to them.

Alan was soon after the December 1942 breakthrough sent him to the United States. He was supposed to meet intelligence officials from the USA and give them instruction on how to build bombes. Also, he was to brief them on the Enigma machine and other German machines. Alan was also given the opportunity to view the progress of an American program that sought to decode cryptic recordings.

Alan returned home to Bletchley and began his research on cryptography in March 1943. He invented "Delilah", which was a speech-scrambling device. Two months later, Alan returned to Bletchley Park to continue his research on cryptography. Although we haven't produced a unit that can do this, the same unit can serve both de-scrambler as well as scrambler. It changes between them by throwing a switch. The unit uses seven valves. If rearranged correctly, it will probably take up approximately 10x8x5 ...". This device was activated only once, scrambling Winston Churchill's speeches. But, it was never used during WW2.

Bletchley Park's penetration of the Enigma computer and the associated codes gave Bletchley Park ULTRA intelligence. This information influenced the Battle of the Atlantic. It also influenced the wars of North Africa, the Mediterranean, West Europe and North Africa in many ways. In the meantime, Germans also penetrated British codes. This enabled them to predict Atlantic convoy movements and make them vulnerable against attacks by U.boat "wolfpacks."

The Germans relentlessly harassed shipping carrying war supplies to Britain via the United States and Canada during the first half. Churchill feared for the survival of the "Scepter'd Isle" when the Kriegsmarine increased the number of losses. However, the convoy system enabled enough shipping to make it through to keep Britain alive in the fight. This was despite the loss of much tonnage and many lives. In the Hobbesian world, rescues from sunken merchantmen were rare and almost always by chance.

As ULTRA cryptography improved, sea lanes became safer and more reliable for the convoys that provided England with its lifeline. Other technologies were also used to aid in this task, including radar and sonar. Sub-hunting aircraft such as U.S.S. were introduced after the Americans entered the war. Bogue, who had been a successful submarine hunter, but whose keel was built by a merchantman named Steel Advocate, began to pay a heavy price from the U.boats. Even Americans used dirigibles for anti-submarine purposes.

The U-boat fleet's success rate increased for a time after the "Shark Blackout," in 1942, which was followed by the October coup at Port Said by three brave British seafarers. U-boat operations were especially vulnerable to encryption because they had been centrally controlled. Karl Donitz (Kriegsmarine Head) controlled all information on weather, ship movements, and so forth. Constant Enigma signals were then sent back-and-forth between the U boats and the Kriegsmarine headquarter.

Donitz anticipated a massacre when 18 major convoys sailed that month in January 1943. The juicy prize never came to pass. Donitz's U.boats explored the oceans without success. British and American vessels were absent everywhere they went. The German naval chief was shocked by this remarkable failure. It seemed that the convoys knew precisely where the U boat's intended location was and so they sailed to avoid them. Donitz wrote a memorandum that stated the situation. (Budiansky2000.290).

An extensive investigation followed, and the Germans couldn't find any traitors at the Kriegsmarine signals corps. The Kriegsmarine also reviewed information about U-boat signals as well as the rate at which they succeeded in intercepting convoys. Although they correctly analyzed the information, the men were unable to draw correct conclusions. They found that not all U.boat-convoy attacks ended in failure. During the war, there were no Allied attempts at decoding codes that had a 100% success rates. This was due to decryption rates as low or high as 50%. Some messages remained undeciphered by bombers and cryptoanalysis experts for several hours, with no decoded version available until it was too late.

The Germans also observed that British sailors continued to use their existing naval codes, which had been broken long ago by Third Reich experts. This was actually not due to a lack Enigma information, as the Germans thought, but rather a bureaucratic error. The Kriegsmarine ignored the fact that their enemies were competent in breaking Enigma codes. Instead, they underestimated their competence in managing their code secrecy.

On March 16, 1943, the Uboats got a last shot at life when a fleet of 40 German subs attacked two convoys. The submarines sank 22 merchantmen along with one escort. The U'boats were quickly driven to port by the addition of 4-inch wavelength anti-submarine radar and renewed efforts from ULTRA.

Donitz maintained his conviction that the British couldn't decrypt the messages. This was almost comical. Donitz sent signals speculated that the English had created infrared imagery technology. The British "confirmed" their suspicions by feeding the Kriegsmarine misinformation through several well-placed doubles agents. The U-boats had to be refitted quickly with anti infrared detection paint. The paint reflected the 4-inch wavelength of radar far better than the Uboat hull. This made the signature of the U.S. vessels stand out against the background "noise."

Even in the rare instances when the British could not prevent an event from occurring, they often used ULTRA information to make German victory more expensive. The British defenses received detailed deployment information as well as advance warning of the Germans' May 1941 invasion of Crete.

Although too outnumbered to prevent the island's fall the British and New Zealand commanders inflicted heavy losses on Germans. Hitler would never authorize major

Fallschirmjager Paratroop Insertions again. The "Green Devils", fighting as elite infantry, deprived Third Reich's war machine of tactical options offered by vertical envelopement, were then reformed to be the Third Reich's elite infantry.

ULTRA intercepts helped the Allied commanders to see the strategic movements of the Axis throughout the whole land war. ULTRA signals revealed, for example that the Germans believed D-Day landing sites in Normandy provided an unlikely spot for attack. Instead, they concentrated their most powerful defenses near Calais.

ULTRA's immense value was again demonstrated by the British, and the Americans, when the Allied forces arrived at the coast and advanced through France. Hitler ordered Gunther Von Kluge, his long suffering subordinate to, to conduct a massive counterattack against Mortain mid-August. He was to lead 15 divisions as part of an effort to destroy American forces breaking out of Normandy. Kluge considered his effort futile and tried unsuccessfully to convince Hitler to stop pursuing the plan.

Bletchley Park's frantic cryptanalysis crew decrypted Hitler's entire exchange with Kluge in less than an hour. It gave the Americans four more days to prepare a deadly trap against the Wehrmacht counterattack. This involved attacking an advancing force from the sides, and then using Patton's troops for an encirclement maneuver. F.W. Winterbotham, a RAF Intelligence Officer, later recalled how "at first light, 4th Panzer Division roared to the little town Mortain through forward American roadblocks. Their extraordinary momentum carried them seven-miles beyond the town, before the Allied planes came after them. Quesada's fighter bombers as well the British Typhoons with their rockets must be a blunder on the unaware panzers. Then they ran into Bradley's massed armillery. "The German tanks could not be stopped." (Winterbotham, 1974, 152).

Between August 12th-21st, the Allies beat the German forces trapped within what became the Falaise Pocket. 10,000 Germans died in the process of covering the ground with dead flesh. Eisenhower reported that for hundreds and even miles, the soil surface appeared invisible below a layer of human remains. Kluge's final reserves were destroyed when 50,000 more surrendered. It also cost the Germans many irreplaceable Panzers including Panzer V Panthers.

Hitler was a fool for ordering the counterattack from remote headquarters without knowing local conditions. However, rapid ULTRA cryptography of his and Kluge's orders transformed the idea in to a disaster of the Wehrmacht's and a triumphant ambush by the Allies.

ULTRA techs correctly detected and analyzed the Germans' Ardennes Offensive preparations, despite high security. The same conclusion was reached independently by Colonel Oscar Koch of Patton's intelligence, who used only prisoners and aerial reconnaissance to arrive at the same conclusion.

Oscar Koch

Despite this, the attack came off harder than expected. However, the American 101st Airborne remained at Bastogne and delayed the advance by occupying crucial road junctions. ULTRA intercepted a signal saying Antwerp couldn't be reached, and informed Eisenhower (and the rest of Allied high Command) of the defeat by Hitler's final major offensive to the West.

General Dwight D. Eisenhower praised ULTRA at Bletchley Park and all its members for their outstanding efforts just two months before war was over.

While Alan receives the majority of credit, it's important for us to not forget the contributions made by Joan Clarke, a mathematics major who was taken up by Welchman June 1940. Welchman had been impressed by Joan Clarke's ability for crunching numbers. He enthusiastically supported Joan for the role of candidate and once stated that he was as good as any of his fellow Cambridge University professors.

Joan was inducted into the clerical staff and, like her male counterparts, received a measly average L2 per workweek. In just two short weeks, Hut 8's top officials found her talents and set her up with them an additional station. Thus, she was the only woman in a male-dominated, nine-member Banburist group. Her role was important, but emotionally draining. She was responsible for decoding ciphers in real-time alongside her colleagues. This was crucial because thousands would depend on her actions.

While she was working, the pressure she felt must not have affected her "congenial...shy...and] gentle" disposition. She was more meticulous than her male colleagues. She was also very conscientious and could often be found waiting for hours to double-check and playing with different calculations in hopes of finding a good solution. It would have been fair to give her a proper raise. But, as the law forbids her from earning equal earnings to male colleagues, Alan made Joan monolingual and promoted her to "Linguist".

Joan was already close friends with Alan, Hut 8's director, by the spring of 1941. Their dedication to each other and their mutual diligence only strengthened their friendship. Joan later recalled that Alan came in every day for a day's leave. He was doing his mathematical research in the office in the warmth.

The couple soon fell in love and Alan made every effort to make sure their schedules coincided. This allowed them to spend more time together. Joan was, to Alan, a bright and brilliant individual whose intellect surpassed his. They shared a few common interests, including a love for chess. Alan often brought a battered cardboard pocket set from home to entertain them. To replace the pieces they'd lost throughout the years, they made their own out of clay from a nearby mine.

Alan might have been a bachelor. But he was not necessarily eligible in the traditional sense. Cawthorne stated, "Sometimes Alan appeared in the office dressed in his pajamas and/or wore trousers that were held up by a striped necktie rather than a belt." His hair was long and unmanaged. He also had a five o'clock shadow that he refused shaving with anything except an old electric razor. He didn't smoke and his teeth looked yellow. Bletchley employees noticed his oddities and were not surprised. The little-faced genius rode to work every day with a bulky gas mask attached to his face. This was to stop seasonal allergies. Alan was unable to afford to repair his damaged chain or replace the rusty bike. Instead, he worked out exactly when his chain would break and then dismounted the bike in record time. The notoriously messy mathematician had excessive concerns over little things. Alan kept his teacup firmly attached to his radiator in his office to discourage thieves.

Alan, a very underrated runner who once was close to qualifying to the British Olympic team by running 11 minutes faster than his competitors, would often sprint to work all day and beat those who commuted. It was difficult to miss his pungent body odor. This was an inevitable result of his constant running. Alan confessed that "I have such an stressful job that running hard is my only way to get out of it." This is the only way I can find some relief.

Joan loved Alan deeply, and it was clear that she was very fond of her friendship. Alan proposed abruptly to Joan, even presenting a fine-silver band to her. Joan remembered the disclaimer Alan added to his proposal. Joan spoke about it in an interview many decades later. Alan softly replied, "But...I must tell you." Joan did not even notice the comment. It was hard to believe that Joan could have homosexual tendencies. Joan decided to accept it and move on. This move might seem confusing today, but in the early 20th Century, mutual sexual pleasure was not considered part of some marriages. A lifetime of platonic companionship was enough for her.

Joan chose to not reveal her hand at work to avoid false rumors concerning special treatment. This could have jeopardized her position at Bletchley. However, the pair seemed to have taken their unconsummated relationship very seriously for some time. Joan was already acquainted with Ethel when Alan was introduced by Mrs. Clarke. The "couple" discussed their future and Alan expressed his desire for children.

Alan did not doubt that Joan was his greatest love, but he found it impossible to change his core. Joan would not be able to have a man who could care for her in the same way he could. They split about a full year later, but remained close friends up until the end.

The Apple

"We can only view a very short distance ahead, but can see plenty that is necessary." - Alan Turing

Alan, unlike any other actor, is three-dimensional. He is often seen on silver screen as a cynical nervous character who is unable to control his emotions. Despite his quirks (and his brutal honesty), which were certainly irritating to those around him at times; the man seemed to care deeply about his coworkers, even subordinates. Mike Coodger (personal assistant to Alan at Bletchley) fell ill with glandular flu just a few short weeks after his first shift. He was prepared to be reprimanded and disciplined by his short-tempered superior. Instead, he discovered this note on the desk of his superior.

"Dear Woodger,

"Unfortunately Wilkinson & I have both arranged that we go on leave... I think you can keep yourself quite busy though. You could.

Do ROOT, and OUTPUT

Volunteer to assist others in Division who are doing ACE jobs.

Take a look at the folder.

Take a look at a great book.

Relax.

"I trust you are doing well. It is very disappointing to see you return and find the area deserted. You might consider a relapse of a week.

Yours,

Alan Turing."

Alan was well aware that his brilliance was obvious, but he was also uncomfortable with being the center of attention. The OBE (Order of the British Empire), medal he received from King George VI for his service in the war was a prized possession that he kept until his death. However, one of Alan's coworkers took the initiative to add the distinction plaque to Alan's office door. He reportedly flew into an angry fit.

Turing's OBE, now stored in the Sherborne School Archives

Alan was born in Richmond, SW London and moved there in 1946. In Richmond, he was employed by the National Physical Laboratory. He was able, then, to enhance his already-designed Automatic Computing Engine (ACE), which would be the first electronic store-program and computer in the world. While the Turing Machine is merely a theoretical machine, the ACE is London's "physical computer". The ACE was Europe's "general purpose" machine.

Alan, giddy with his proposal for building the ACE, presented it to the executive committee of laboratory towards the end 1945. The project was estimated at L11,000. Charles Darwin was the grandson of Darwin and the current head of NPL. He immediately noticed his proposal, and discussed the possibility of making the project more prominent and making it national. However, the project was ultimately scrapped due to its high cost.

Alan spent less than a year at NPL but the impression he left on his fellow workers was profound. Robin Addie noted that Alan wanted to develop active elements for his computer projects. His vivid memories of him include a man medium in build, with crew-cut, round hair, and bent over what was described as an "electric bird's nest" of resistors. Turing just wanted ..." to fix all the components.